MIKE PENCE & ME

Bryan O'Nolan

Copyright © 2023 Bryan O'Nolan

All rights reserved

The characters and events portrayed in this book are fictitious. Any similarity to real persons, living or dead, is coincidental and not intended by the author.

No part of this book may be reproduced, or stored in a retrieval system, or transmitted in any form or by any means, electronic, mechanical, photocopying, recording, or otherwise, without express written permission of the publisher.

ISBN-13: 9798850544980

Cover design by: Kevin Fox
Library of Congress Control Number: 2018675309
Printed in the United States of America

CONTENTS

Title Page

Copyright

Dedication

Epigraph

The Time Mike's Woody Was Full of Hookers	1
The Time Mike & the 23rd Indiana Light Artillery Castrated a Bull	8
The Day that Comprised the Totality of Mike's Bare Knuckle Boxing Career	16
The Time Mike Caused $135,000 in Damage at His Local Target	24
The Time Mike Ate the World's Hottest Pepper	32
The Time Mike Took Me to the Gathering of the Juggalos	40
The Time Mike Went on an Ayahuasca-Fueled Vision Quest	49
Whatever Became of Dora the Explorer?	58

The Time Mike Killed an Endangered Bald Eagle	71
The Time That Mike Encountered a Wendigo & I Introduced Him to the Future Mrs. Michael Pence	81
The Time Mike Foiled a Jesuit Conspiracy to Infiltrate & Seize New Brunswick	92
the Time Mike Foiled a Jesuit Conspiracy to Infiltrate & Seize New Brunswick	101
The Time Mike Squandered Three Wishes Granted by a Crone	110
The Time Mike Prevented a Shark from Beheading a Moose	119
The Time Mike Pence Saved Christmas	130
The Time That Booper & I Exfiltrated Mike Pence From Cuba	138
The Time Mike Pence Just Shot a Man in the Face	149
Booper McCarthy & the Great Chicken Truck Rescue	159
From Piles to Piracy	167
Booper McCarthy and the Unquiet Shade of Salubrity Prescott	185
Where Waldo Was	202
Mike's First Foray Into Politics	223
The Time Booper & I Lost the Pence Children at the County Fair	236

The Time Mike Tried to Make Scottishness Great Again 250

A Victory of Illogic, A Comedy of Errors 261

Introduction

I have known Bryan O'Nolan for over twenty years, since the late '90s or so. They say that sometimes you meet a person and immediately realize they are destined for greatness. Meeting Bryan was nothing like that. All you knew was that he was destined for strangeness. He once super-glued a frozen pea to a wall in college to see what would happen.

Well, It stuck.

So when he told me he had this idea for a series of stories which were simultaneously about and *not* about then-Vice President Mike Pence, I knew it was going to be strange. I began getting scraps of ideas, sketches, strange snatches of dialogue in dialect in my email.

Scattered, stream-of-consciousness flashes.

"Mike gets drunk. Pastor Dennis busts him. Mike curses for the first time."

"Mike fails to realize his roommate is gay."

I don't know if much of my feedback, or what served as feedback when I could make sense of what I was reading, influenced the final product, but I know that eventually Bryan proposed the series to the folks at Ordinary Times. What they made of it initially, we may never know. But I do know that I got an excited email with thirteen hundred or so words of typical O'Nolanian nonsense about Mike Pence, rugby and prostitutes which eventually made its way to publication.

What you have here is that and all that followed it. Bryan, who is not quite the real Bryan, telling stories of Mike, who is not the real Mike, and Booper, who Bryan tells me is based on a real person no longer with us, and their strange adventures. The tension between reality and absurdity is tightly wrought. I know that Bryan has felt frustrated and challenged by our late reality's sudden willingness to venture into the country of the absurd it had hitherto been content to leave thinly explored.

Early on I tried to get a handle on what all of this was, what all of it meant. Bryan's answer was vague, but he spoke of the difference between a public figure's persona and the complex reality behind it. He specifically mentioned the idea that a persona we call Mike Pence might have been in the background of the cult hit film *Heavy Metal Parking Lot* without changing who the person behind the persona is. There's a passing reference to this, but I think the clearest example is when Mike takes Bryan to the Gathering of the Juggalos.

Why Mike? I suppose he is someone that the American public can agree upon, as far as his essential elements of his character. If we can separate our opinion of the man from that character, most of us can probably come to an agreement on who the man is. Many other public figures, such as Mike's former boss, could not create such a consensus, or near-consensus. But Mike is a relatively straight forward figure.

To take this straight forward figure and place him in situations which appear to be incongruous to his character, and yet have him step out of them unsullied is contrary to "gotcha" culture and "cancel" culture.

Bryan and I have often discussed whether or not our culture allows us to have heroes anymore, or if they must be shown to be as base and tainted as we are. Perhaps, in this collection, we're being offered one: a folk-hero bizzarro-world Mike Pence.

Bryan has asked me to write this because, I suppose, more than anyone else I'd seen the behind the scenes thinking. I don't suppose he realized that what qualified as "behind the scenes thinking" involved supergluing a frozen pea to a wall, a theoretical invention of something called "Phenobarbasol" and twenty years of oddly and widely referential humor.

The very notion of "behind the scenes" and "thinking" were being challenged without him having the least awareness.

I suppose the quintessential Bryan O'Nolan story is this: In the early years of this century he and his father and I were watching a B-movie. At one point, the two female leads got into a fight. When the aggressor regained her senses, she said to her counterpart, "I'm sorry for my coarse remark."

We found this hysterical.

It was an oft-quoted in-joke for years.

Eventually, Bryan tracked the film down, only to discover that we'd misheard the line so many years later.

Did it bother him?

Not at all.

It had stuck.

Coel Hen, June 2023

Author's note: But for the last, the stories below were first published in the online magazine Ordinary Times. The dates included are either the date of publication or the date of completion.

I am extremely thankful to the editors of Ordinary Times for taking a flier on a you-kinda-had-to-be-there concept.

THE TIME MIKE'S WOODY WAS FULL OF HOOKERS

The following story is meant to be humorous, and is not intended to represent the real-life Mike Pence. As far as we know he did not, in fact, do this.

Sometimes Mike Pence's trademark friendliness and humility would land us in some strange situations. A perfect example of this happened after we'd graduated from college. We'd joined an amateur rugby club called Peonies R.F.C. Mike was our fly-half and easily the best damn fly-half I've ever seen, to beat the band. It was almost unfair, our go-to play, the way he'd take the feed from Dick Richards, our scrum-half, bolt around the scrum and be over the try line before you could say Albert Pell.

I was a barely passable full-back, but a

wizard with the athletic tape. Still am to this day.

One warm Saturday afternoon we had a fixture against our greatest rival, Thrips. I think I will encounter no meaningful rebuttal if I suggest that Thrips were the meanest pack of brigands and ruffians you could ever encounter on the rugby pitch. High tackling. Offsides by miles. Genitals grabbed at every opportunity. Fouls the like of which have not been seen on a rugby pitch before. These were the gentlemen, you understand, against whom we were called into action on that fateful Saturday.

Mike and myself arrived at the pitch in his sun-faded orange woody van — yclept Woody, naturally — ready in our togs and raring for the fight of our lives. We met up with Richards and our self-declared captain Romney and the rest of the squad, except there was a serious problem. Dick Richards, our number two, was sick with the mononucleosis and could in no way play. A fine kettle of fish: A Thrips fixture and Dick with the kissing disease. Please understand, we were a two-bit, bootstraps, sweat off the old brow outfit that couldn't field a side with a player missing. We could field a substitute as soon as a submarine.

However — so importantly to the old spirit of the club — we weren't about to be sidelined and forfeited by such a gang of ne'er do wells as Thrips. Many's the side we might have reluctantly forfeited to, shaken hands and good on you for your success, but against these characters such was not an option.

Captain Romney gathered us together, scrum like.

Now, Michael, Romney said. We all know you're a reliable, resourceful man. I don't think I'm mistaken in nominating you, Mr. Michael Pence, to find for us a replacement for a sadly absent member of this august body, Peonies R.F.C. No rugby team is complete without a number two, and Mr. Dick Richards has tucked his ears back and, boy howdy, served as our able hooker for as long as I can remember. He is, I understand, indisposed with a health concern which may have resulted from a romantic encounter, albeit, I assume, a chaste one. I am sure that you, Mike, can find a suitable replacement, and preferably within the next hour.

So officiously was it intoned and so it was to be done.

Off we sped in the old woody, like men on fire, though like men on fire who were driven by one who religiously adhered to the posted speed limit. Mike had some sermons of Pastor Dennis's on 8-track that we listened to which kept our minds engaged as he drove.

We were a long way from home and in parts unknown and Mike took the first off ramp once we hit a municipality of any size. He pulled into a parking lot likely enough and rolled down his window.

There was a wide expanse of parked long

haul truckers, great fields of idle diesel and freight. A man of some considerable girth sat in a dilapidated lawn chair drinking out of a styrofoam cup like he was their king.

Hello, friend, Mike said. We're from Peonies Rugby Club. We have a match today and I'm in need of the best hooker you can find.

I sank low in my seat in a vain attempt at invisibility.

Wellsir, quoth His Highness. Every man has his own, shall we say, interests. Predilections. Disgustibus, as the old fella said. But there's a fine selection down behind the lime green Peterbilt with the dry box, yonder.

Thank you so very much, sir, Mike said.

Catch you on the flip flop, Rubber Duckie, the sweaty king said with a lazy salute.

Mike rolled up his window.

Mike, said I, I don't know that that man's quite understood exactly what we were looking for.

How so? Mike asked.

Well, I suggested, there are other meanings of the word "hooker," for starters.

Oh no, Bryan, Mike said. While I understand the regrettable level of attention Rugby Union gets in this country — you know? I've considered running for political office to address just this very problem — but I will not prejudge these men based simply on their profession and perceived lack of social standing.

We found the Peterbilt, a loud lime green number festooned with a cross on its grill which appeared to be fashioned out of 100 Watt light bulbs.

See? he said. A God-fearing truck driver. You must have more faith in your fellow man, Bryan!

We stepped out of Woody and walked to the back of the trailer. We heard giggling. There was a smell of cigarettes and other combustibles. Coarse language seasoned the air. Somewhere nearby, a glass bottle was rolling along the asphalt. We turned at the end of the trailer and there, in the back of the empty dry box, were a half dozen women who could only be prostitutes. Fishnets and bosomflesh for days.

I confess I cleared my throat.

Mike turned to me.

Bryan, he said, I owe you the sincerest of my apologies.

A blonde at the front inquired as to what, you understand, services we required and briefly quoted us a price for the renderation of the various services aforesaid.

Ladies, said Mike, there has been an enormous misunderstanding. My friend and I are members of an amateur rugby club. One of the key positions on the team is our number two, also known as a hooker. Ours is sick today and we needed a replacement—

I get it. I understand, a dark beauty at the back said. I think I can help you out.

No! We're not looking for anything, er, untoward, we just—

Shut it, man! You're wanting me brother, Paul. Paul! she called.

I couldn't help myself.

What is going on? I asked. I don't understand a damned thing.

From around the front end of the truck came a stout lad with long, curled black hair and muscles that challenged his shirt's capacity to contain them.

We're in real danger now, I thought, but Mike's face was more inquisitive than fearful.

Tell him what you're looking for, man, the dark beauty barked.

We, sir, Mike said. Are in need of a hooker.

This man — Paul, as it turned out — broke into a wide smile.

You've found your lad, then! Where's the match? he cried.

Not five minutes later Paul, his sister Sheila and the other ladies — hookers, all — had piled into the back of Woody and we were on our way back to the match. Turns out Paul played for Saracens for a few years and even won two caps for Fiji. A brave, stout lad. Solid number two. No one complained about the sermons of Pastor Dennis on the 8-track.

Paul was a perfect fit for our system. Brilliant in the breakdown and a master of the line out. He was the key to our famous defeat of Thrips that day. The scoreline was an embarrassment, but the fact that we took our feet off the gas in the last third of the match just to be sporting made it even moreso.

As for the ladies, I can report that all of them made their way to Jesus, each in her own way, after that day. Three of them became Elementary school teachers, two run faith-based day care centers and, well, I won't embarrass Sister Mary Michael by revealing her current location but, suffice it to say, she has changed her ways.

❊ ❊ ❊

Sometime I have to tell you about the time Mike shot the family dog in front of the children.

2nd May, 2020

THE TIME MIKE & THE 23RD INDIANA LIGHT ARTILLERY CASTRATED A BULL

The following story is meant to be humorous, and is not intended to represent the real-life Mike Pence. As far as we know he has not, in fact, formulated a proof of Fermat's Last Theorem.

Many people carry a little something around with them at all times. A sort of *vade mecum*, if you will. It could be devotional, talismanic or practical; a Rosary, a rabbit's foot or a multi-tool. For Mike Pence — and few people know this, mind — it's a unique class of knife. How this came to be, of course, is a snorter of a story. Don't read this standing up; the publisher says he will not be responsible for any injuries that may be imputed to this book.

When Mike was fifteen, he suffered a catastrophic ski jumping accident which resulted in a compound fracture of a femur. I won't be telling that story as it's rather graphic, but suffice it to say it involved several bison and a half dozen Mounties covered in blood. As a result, he was laid up all winter and boredom crept in, as it does.

He called me one day.

Bryan, he said. I am bored.

But, Mike, I said. You were going to work on a proof of Fermat's Last Theorem. It's only been three weeks!

I was and I did, he said. And let me tell you, Bryan, you'd need a margin as wide as this great nation to fit the beast.

Are you going to submit it for publication in some scholarly journal? I asked.

He only laughed.

No, no. This knowledge is of no practical benefit to our fellow man. I sought it only as a whetstone for the mind in my isolation. What I need now is some reading material, and I think you're just the fellow to procure it for me.

Mike, I said. You're so widely read that I don't know just what to get you.

I think biography is a safe genre, he replied. The lives of great men may be an inspiration or a cautionary tale. To me, they will be a comfort in my convalescence.

Well, it was as I spied his house on my walk home from school the next day that I remembered, so I doubled back to the public library. I grabbed a swathe of books which, through a pure accident of the Dewey Decimal System, was comprised entirely of biographies of commissioners of Major League Baseball.

Thus, three years later, we found ourselves spending Spring Break with our fellow Civil War reenactors — we were the 23rd Indiana Light Artillery, you understand — participating in a reenactment of the Battle of Kennesaw Mountain.

It was a fine April morning.

The air was clean and crisp and the unit woke to muster at our position just near a hobby farm.

Our buddy Gregg Hoff was checking out our 3-inch Ordnance Rifle which, despite the name, was a class of small cannon. (Incidentally, Gregg was the drummer in a locally popular punk outfit you may have heard of called Lord Smudge and the Tonetones). The rifle was an 800 pound wrought iron gentleman with a great chthonic boom that could liquefy the contents of your bowels. Don't ask me how I know; I've no doubt you could guess and hit near enough to the mark yourself, being an urbane and thoughtful reader.

Mike was very invested in the mythology

of the thing, Sherman's army and the battlefield and Shoeless Joe Jackson and all sorts of old timey nonsense I couldn't for the life of me follow. I was more interested — and could not have been more disappointed — in the prospect of camp followers. I pointed out early in the campaign that nearly 90% of the casualties suffered by the real 23rd died of disease and that while he and Hoff and the rest were off play fighting I'd be pretending to be on my deathbed. This, of course, looked suspiciously like sleeping in, or so I was told.

So it was that bright morning that I lay in my cot playing my usual part: Minding my own business, thoughtfully considering the inside of my eyelids whilst putting on a brave face fighting a losing battle against gangrene, cholera, dysentery, the English sweat or — on a certain occasion during a cold, windy and rainy rendition of the Battle of Resaca — the black death.

I liked to keep my options plentiful.

That morning it was the yellow fever.

I remember it distinctly, the tent fluttered in the gentle, Georgia breeze. Somewhere a cock crowed. Flies buzzed about the beans that'd been my breakfast. And then the morning was broken by an unholy explosion, a boom so sudden and so loud that I flopped out of my cot and nearly opened my chest cavity on the razor sharp lid of the can of beans aforesaid.

I burst out of the tent to discover

untempered chaos. Hoff was stumbling about near the cannon in a daze. The rifle had kicked back and rolled over someone's foot, the someone in question now rolling in the high grass in exquisite pain. Several shelter halves had been flattened by men running away from the blast. Some of our infantry down the line thought the battle had started and were charging a unit of Confederates beyond who were waking in complete ignorance that their position was about to be overrun.

Somehow, in checking the 3-inch in the early morning idleness, drummer Hoff had fired it off.

Our unit was a shambles, but the real chaos came from the adjacent farm. Above the animal noises was a shout of people calling for help. We rushed over. A tempest of chickens fluttered about. A goat bleated madly. Worst of all, the farmer, his right arm in a cast from his wrist to his shoulder, ran out of the barn in a panic.

Estelle! the farmer cried. Our Estelle is calving! The cannon blast put her in labor!

Mike and I were the first on the scene. Mike put his hands on the mother's belly.

Gosh dang it, Bryan, this calf is not in the proper position! he said. Do you have gloves, good farmer?

The farmer confessed that he had none.

Mike, unperturbed, brought himself around to the rear of the laboring heifer. I will spare you, dear reader, the most gruesome details, but the calf was, through Mike's messy and rather penetrative intervention, brought around and delivered into the world. The calf didn't appear to be breathing so Mike sucked at the poor thing's snout to get it started.

Many would call the sight of mother and calf a beautiful thing, and I'll allow it may be so, but I found it stomach churning, in this case.

Bryan, Mike said, absently putting his arm — itself covered in blood and viscera and God knows what else — around my shoulder. I fought the impulse to vomit. The reason she eats the afterbirth is that, were she in the wild, the scent could attract predators.

That was it. Technical terms had been used. The partially digested contents of the can of beans rose violently up into my throat and I vomited like I never have before or since.

Another issue, however, presented itself: You see, the calf was male.

What plans have you for his, shall we say, disposition? Mike asked.

I suppose I'll need to have him fixed, even though, strictly speaking, he's not broken, the farmer replied with a feeble laugh.

Well then, when will you be castrating the poor lad? asked Mike.

This is the first time I've dealt with this, sir, the farmer said. I frankly have no idea.

There is no consensus when it comes to the timing of the castration, Mike said. However, from what I understand from my travels in America's dairyland, the best intervention is an early one.

And what does the literature say regarding the question of banding versus cutting? the farmer asked.

I admit there's as little consensus there as there is regarding the timing, Mike said. But, as I see that you have two beautiful little girls, I recommend the knife. Banding results in the eventual sloughing off of the testicle-laden scrotum and many consider this unsightly.

The farmer agreed.

There was a great confusion of searching and, after several minutes, a Newberry Knife of questionable sharpness was produced. It was found in the family junk drawer, though none could ascertain how it had found its way there. Mike looked dubiously at the instrument, a dull and rusty fellow. He'd need all the strength in the forearms he could muster to geld this lily in one go.

A deep breath and a quick prayer heavenward and our man had himself steadied. Before you knew it he had a pair of newly freed bovine testicles in his left hand and a broad smile of relief on his face.

To this day, Mike carries a sharpened Newberry Knife about with him at all times, just in case.

Sometime I should tell you about the

summer Mike and I spent as lighthouse keepers in Downeast Maine and foiled a Jesuit conspiracy.

9th May 2020

THE DAY THAT COMPRISED THE TOTALITY OF MIKE'S BARE KNUCKLE BOXING CAREER

The following story is meant to be humorous, and is not intended to represent the real-life Mike Pence. As far as we know he has never, in fact, been to Bondi Beach.

It was at a rest stop outside of Dayton, Ohio that the hunger kicked in. Mike Pence and I were with our roommate Dick Richards buying snack foods and beverages, completely unaware that several hours before we'd been filmed in the background of the film *Heavy Metal Parking Lot*.

Our good friend Dick has always been an impulsive guy; he'd happily admit this to you.

It was as he was about to pay — it was his turn, this stop — when he said, Hey, I'll take a Number 6. And before we knew it the cashier was ripping off a scratch ticket.

Two months later we found ourselves trekking the Australian Outback.

Mike, being Mike, took a great interest in the plight of the aboriginal people of that continent. He asked often after their ways and their legal status in Australia. Dick wanted to tour the beaches. For myself, I just wanted to see a kangaroo. So Mike, Dick and I ended up going to an outfitter who promised to take us into the interior. Brent McGillicuddy was the name attached to his gruff, weathered person. He and Dick became fast friends.

Several days in, it got to be evening and we'd found a likely enough spot to set up camp. Just as we were about to begin supper we heard the panicked screams of a woman: My baby! My baby! she cried. We ran to her at once.

We found the mother and her two other children frantic. Mike was calm, and calming.

Ma'am, we are here to help, he said.

Was it a dingo? I couldn't help but ask. Mike glared at me. I patted my brow dry with my handkerchief.

It just appeared, she said. Out of nowhere. And before we knew it, it had grabbed Alphonse and was gone!

We will begin a search at once, Mike said. First you must let us know when and in what approximate direction your baby may have gone.

But, was. It. A. Dingo? I demanded.

Bryan, Mike said.

One who knew him, as I did, would be attuned to the minute change in the tone of his voice that communicated rather clearly that one had grossly overstepped one's bounds.

Why don't you go and fetch our flashlights and lanterns and — he said as he grabbed me by the arm — grab as many batteries as you can.

I was off at a run. I know when I've been put in me place and I'm not the sort to make it worse by fussing, so I collected the lanterns, flashlights, batteries and a first aid kit and stuffed them in a rucksack I'd emptied by dumping it out on the ground. I will say I was surprised at the depth of our friend Richards' interest in men's fashion by the voluminous ...volume of reading material on the subject that came out, piled high on the dusty ground.

By the time I got back to the group, Mike had all the details he needed and McGillicuddy was ready to help us track the baby, or whatever had it.

Mike, I whispered. Was it—?

No, he said quietly. A kangaroo.

I was torn between a thrill of excitement and a paroxysm of fear. On the one hand, I might finally get to see my kangaroo. On the other hand...

Mike, I said. I'm told your kangaroos are some of the fiercest, most unpleasant, most disputatious gentlemen you can meet in God's beautiful creation.

We have to chance it, Bryan, he said. There's a child's life in the balance.

I'll grant you that, I said, perhaps too loudly. But the kangaroo is — I have it on good authority from the most learned men on the subject of the kangaroo — the most irksome, most disagreeable character walking about under the sun. A personality the equal of which you could only fashion by crossing the disposition of the camel, the wasp and a mule with a nasty infection of the urinary tract. Meet this fellow in a dark alley and if he doesn't like the look of you, he'll donkey-bonk you, arse over tea kettle, into the next month without a care in the world.

But, Bryan, Mike said. I thought you wanted to see one.

His voice — if such a thing is possible — *winked* at me.

See? I said. Yes. At a distance, majestic giant bipedal rabbits that they are. Meet? In person? With it between me and something it coveted? No, thank you. I'd rather be tossed live and whole into a supervolcano, thank you very much. The person of a kangaroo is not one I'd want to find myself in dispute with in a pub, much less in a dispute in his own well-trod back garden.

Have no fear, Bryan, Mike said. We'll rescue

this poor babe from the uncouth clutches of this rude beast.

As usual, I had to take his confidence on as my own.

McGillicuddy, the brave Australian that he was, was tracking that roo brigand in the dark like I could follow an interstate at noon on a bicycle.

Few people know this, but the kangaroo will, under certain conditions, turn a cave into his lair. There he keeps his unholy harem of jills and the sun-baked bones of his slain foes. Oh, and the treasure! Not the kind of treasure you or I would appreciate, mind. But the marsupial is nature's original serial shoplifter. Shiny bits of metal, scraps of cloth, old, weathered pharmacy receipts, perhaps a dented folding chair: the gathered detritus of man's dominion over nature.

So it was that our trail came to its end before the mouth of such a cave. The child, playing absentmindedly with an empty packet of candy cigarettes, appeared unharmed by this fellow we shall call The Collector. And between ourselves and the child The Collector stood, like a pugilist preparing for a title fight. I broke out in a cold sweat, unable to move or speak.

We've come for the child! proclaimed Richards who had, for reasons known only to himself, taken off his shirt.

No, Dick, Mike said. I got us into this, and I mean to get us out of it. Save your steely courage: Should I fall, it will be needed then.

Mike walked up to The Collector; each took the measure of the other. Mike was mere inches taller than his opponent. He squared up manfully.

The boomer took the first swing, a roundhouse Mike parried skillfully before countering with a jab to the chin. Your man the roo ducked it like a champion pugilist. Mike was in for the fight of his life.

They circled each other. Mike tried a skillful one-two, but The Collector hid his face behind raised forearms. Sweat was pouring from Mike's brow while the other fellow danced from foot to foot as cool as you please.

Deftly, the kangaroo kicked some dust into the night air. Mike was temporarily blinded and he staggered back.

Gentlemen! I shouted as I stepped in to separate them. Not sporting. Not sporting at all. You should be ashamed of yourself, Mr. Kangaroo. No excuses, now. Expect to be sanctioned, and consider yourself lucky that it's only that.

I withdrew. I'll accept any result as long as there's fair play.

Mike advanced and landed a flurry of body blows. This was a war of attrition now, as far as Mike was concerned. The roo faded back, but Mike was back on him like a flash.

That's when it happened. Mike was pounding the belly of the great beast when an uppercut like a missile launch went through his chin and skyward. Mike was carried up and off his feet and was out before he hit the ground in a great pile of unconscious American goodness. I swear we thought we'd lost him.

No! Dick shouted. The boomer rounded on us.

The sweat was pouring from my brow, now. I took out my handkerchief. He fixed on me, mere, meek Bryan O'Nolan. Up to me he walked, methodical. I froze, handkerchief frozen, still at the temple as he slowly strode to where I stood. I was a dead man. I said me prayers and commended my soul heavenward.

I could smell his fell breath.

His arm slowly reached to my head. I thought he'd be smothering me at any moment. I called to mind every unconfessed sin I could think of and closed my eyes, begging forgiveness. I didn't want to watch my own brutal end. I was about to be beaten, torn limb from limb, my bones to be picked clean and made into a rude, unholy memorial to my brief, pathetic life.

He — hear me now! — with an almost human tenderness, pawed the handkerchief from my sweating brow. I felt it fall and I opened my eyes to see him contrive with his mouth and paws the handkerchief aforesaid into his pocket.

Now, this next is the most incredible moment.

The Collector, my handkerchief stolen, hopped off into his lair, a merry song on his lips, as if nothing at all had happened.

For a moment a tense, chilled silence held the air.

The child's mother, hesitant at first to be sure, retrieved her son.

Well, Mike's post-concussion syndrome caused us to spend the rest of our visit on Bondi Beach, which at least Dick and I appreciated. Mike spent it in a dark hotel room, shunning the sunlight. Do you know what? He said that in the Southern Hemisphere the dizzy spins in his head went in the other direction, counter-clockwise.

* * *

Sometime I'll have to tell you about the time Mike seriously considered cannibalism.

16th May 2020

THE TIME MIKE CAUSED $135,000 IN DAMAGE AT HIS LOCAL TARGET

The following story is meant to be humorous, and is not intended to represent the real-life Mike Pence. As far as we know he is not, in fact, a master of Aikido.

Most people don't associate Michael Pence, our 48th Vice President, with a swathe of retail destruction the likes of which would impress Genghis Khan himself, but it happened once. The result was a sizable donation to a charity of Target's choice and a summer during which he worked as a volunteer bringing shopping carts in from the parking lot in only the hottest, most uncomfortable weather.

It all started the day I threw out my back

in the grocery store. I'd absentmindedly dropped a can of olives on the floor — imagining myself putting one on each forefinger and each pinky finger and putting on my own production of *Waiting for Godot*, as one does — when I stepped on our friend the can and next thing I know there I am like a slapstick vaudevillian of the olden days after stepping on a banana peel, splayed out and writhing in pain in a pile of goldfish crackers in the main aisle of the store. The end cap had broken my fall and I had, in turn, broken the end cap.

It was upon the second or third recounting of this sad tale that Mike decided he needed to teach me an important lesson in what he called the Situational Awareness. Many's the valuable lessons Mike has taught me over the years and none more useful than the value of the Situational Awareness.

We went to his local Target store. Normally all I'd think about — other than modernist works performed by antipasti — is getting to the part of the store that has what I want in the shortest amount of time, but not so when exercising the Situational Awareness. By the self-checkout, there was a small tower of films in the blueray. Near the apothecary stood a display of shampoo. There was a pallet of bags of dog food. A delicate display of stemware was observed. A great, presumably immovable, mass of bags of flour was, through the employment of the Situational Awareness, noted by ourselves.

It was right by the olives that we cut inward. I'd been commenting to Mike that the part of The Boy in the play is taken by myself when he refocused me.

Be not offended, Mike said, that I interrupt your clever insights regarding modernist theater. But I worry, friend, that your focus may have slipped.

Right he was, of course. Right he was. Fair play and all that. I'd lost me focus and I'm a plain enough man to accept earnest correction when it's warranted and warranted it was.

We took a right at a cardboard tiki bar display in boy's clothing and it was then that I saw a most beautiful thing. There at an intersection of main thoroughfares stood two towers topped with a lintel. They were made of packages of the popular game Jenga — which I'm told is manufactured and sold by the fine, fine people at the Hasbro company — and each was a double tall stack of those packages assembled Jenga-fashion. Spanning the top of the towers was another of their like but laid on its side on a thin piece of wood. Three hundred and twenty four boxes, stacked and beautiful.

Heading into the far corner of the store we saw electronics, a display of patio umbrellas and a kiosk of seed packets.

That's when it happened.

A screaming comes across the store. It has happened before, but there is nothing to compare it to now. We turned and there in the middle of the summer seasonal section was an old woman pointing and screaming to beat the band.

Thief! she cried. Thief!

She pointed at a crude wee gentleman in a black and white hooped shirt with a black mask covering his eyes and a black fedora atop his shaggy head. Mike was after him in an instant.

The thief knocked over the kiosk of seed packets which scattered, a slick explosion on the Formica. Small children slipped and fell, tearing open the packets sending seeds everywhere and making the footing even more precarious. Several of the children appeared to be severely injured, though none, I am told, fatally so.

Mike was hot in his pursuit. Your man knew we were after him and tossed over the umbrellas which smashed on the floor, all cracked plastic, bent metal and wires in search of eyes to poke. An elderly gentleman had an artery sliced open by the sharp metal and blood was spouting out of his arm and into an upturned umbrella like he was the Lady Gratton drinking fountain in Stephen's Green.

I followed the chase into the electronics section. Loathe was I to watch what happened there. Displays were mere chaotic piles as the pursuer and his pursued had seen fit to go both over and through the department. Consoles and locked cabinets leaned one against the other like fallen dominoes. Phones and tablets dangled from their displays like a thousand lonely wilted flowers left embarrassed in the sight of the eyes of the world. In the center of what had been the department stood a shell shocked clerk with the thousand-yard stare of an ambulance driver at the Somme.

What happened next was worse. The burglar took a tight turn through Jengahenge. He miscalculated his angle, however, and a single Jenga log was knocked to the floor. Mike was through before the worst happened. The tower began to teeter, the lintel began to slide and the complete collapse of the structure caused a class of sound that even stopped the burglar and Mike in their tracks.

There was silence as all the witnesses stared at the great pile of Jenga pieces. People stood mouths agape. Somewhere a child softly wept into his mother's skirts.

Mike turned to the burglar.

You brigand, he said. You gosh darn monster!

The pursuit resumed, as the burglar, sputtering and flailing, crushed the cardboard tiki bar in his haste. I eyed the olives as they ran past but they remained undisturbed.

Knife! I heard Mike shout. He has a knife!

Then I saw the blade. The burglar stopped and cut a large X in the stack of flour bags, sending their contents onto the floor before he ran off. The ruse worked, at least for a moment, as Mike slipped and careened into the stacked bags which did him the injustice of exploding, fogging the air with its dusty contents. The dust went everywhere and coated the lungs of all the shoppers caught in that dust storm's path.

I heard the display of stemware crash to the floor before I saw it, so thick was the floured air. What I saw shook me to my very core. Shards of broken glass carpeted the aisle. I grabbed two nearby brooms and, standing upon them like skis, I crossed the glassy pain with minimal discomfort.

What I saw when I got to the pallet of dog food sickened me. The Burglar was standing atop it throwing twenty pound bags of the stuff at Mike, each of which exploded turning the floor into a kibble-studded firmament. Oh, the humanity! Several old women with turned ankles were rolling about on the floor in pain.

The burglar leapt and, grabbing the nearby hair care display on his way down, covered the floor in a slippery sea of silicone free, moisture renewing shampoo. A sadder sight you could not behold.

Mike pursued him, still undaunted. One cannot easily daunt Michael Pence. He may be, in point of fact, undauntable.

The burglar obliterated the kiosk of movies like a linebacker hitting at full tilt the marching band's second flute and when I'd got there I slipped on a copy of a mindless comedy and hit the floor in a dive.

Mike was right behind him, his breath

hot on the burglar's neck. Your man the burglar tripped over his own feet and went down by the self checkout and Mike himself went toppling over and beyond him.

They were both to their feet at the same time, the burglar with knife drawn.

Then it happened.

The burglar went to stab Mike in the abdomen. He adroitly flowed out of the way using his right hand to parry the strike downward. At the same time, his left arm came up under the burglar's chin to control his chest with a firm elbow. The left arm then wrapped around the attacker's arm and hyper-extended the elbow, which caused him to drop the knife. His attacker thus disarmed, Mike dropped to one knee and, with his left arm, threw the off-balance burglar to the ground.

While the burglar was stunned, Mike rolled him onto his chest and pinned him in an arm lock, waiting for the police to arrive.

Michael, I gasped, out of breath, skidding to a halt before the pair. What in the hell was that?

The burglar answered before Mike could.

Munetsuki hiji kime, the burglar said. If I'm not mistaken.

Indeed, ruffian, Mike said. You should always comport yourself as if there is a master of Aikido around to correct you in your misbehavior.

Well, Mike made honest restitution to his local Target and I learned that as much as you think you know a friend, he can still surprise you.

* * *

Sometime I should tell you about the time Mike went on an ayahuasca-fueled vision quest.

23rd May 2020

THE TIME MIKE ATE THE WORLD'S HOTTEST PEPPER

The following story is meant to be humorous, and is not intended to represent the real-life Mike Pence. As far as we know the extent of Mike's knowledge of the lanthanide series is not, in fact, a matter of public record..

One wistful spring break in college Mike Pence and I went on a backpacking tour in Sri Lanka. It helped that Mike is fluent in both the Sinhala and the Vedda, and it was the latter that saved our lives. The whole episode is, if you don't mind, a funny one, I'd like to think.

It starts on a return voyage from a party at some friends of Hoff's at Indiana University Purdue University Indianapolis. He, Richards and myself were in Woody and Mike was performing the critical role of driver, designated.

We got pulled over at one of them what you call Sobriety Checkpoints. Right. The worst sobriety checkpoint selection in the history of Western Civilization, I should think. Mr. Michael Pence, if you don't mind, in that very moment the soberest man on the planet, Pastor Dennis on the 8-track and himself suspected of being under the influence of that most insidious devil: Demon Rum. But selected he was, so he pulled ourselves over and the rest of us gathered at an open window to fully enjoy the spectacularly competent display of sobriety he'd presently make.

Well, your man in blue sure put Mike through his paces. Walking the line. Blowing in tubes. Touching his nose. Reciting the alphabet backwards and forwards. Roadside urination. The works. Mike, all pleasant as you please and smiling to beat the band the entire time. But the policeman, convinced beyond all doubt that our friend was under the influence of the Kill Devil, had one more trick in his pocket. What was this trickery?

Mr. Pence, says he. Would you please recite the lanthanide series — here he paused dramatically — in reverse order of atomic weight?

The cheek of the man!

Well, our man Pence sang a song of his own composition naming them from lutetium to lanthanum with a jaunty little chorus about dysprosium and praseodymium to round the whole thing out. Woody housed an ovation and the policeman, a sour sort of gentleman, begrudgingly ceded the field.

Michael, says I. Why did you learn this particular, obscure information?

Well, he said. I just submitted a paper on the subject to a conference in Sri Lanka. In fact I was hoping you'd accompany me, Bryan.

Sure and don't you know I agreed on the spot.

After the conference we decided to take a few days and do some backpacking in the bush. We'd signed ourselves up with a guide, who'd appeared right and trustworthy enough, a gent by the name of Pasindu Thedsanamoorthy. Well, Pasindu Ted, as he said he should be called, guided us deep into the jungle. He was a great guide at first. He knew by sight and sound which creatures were dangerous and which harmless, which leaf would soothe and which cause a class of diarrhea that would make Montezuma blush. Many's the tale of high adventure and derring-do he regaled us with as we hacked through the leafy jungle.

You can imagine, then, that we had quite a shock on the third day out of Sri Jayawardenepura Kotte. Pasindu Ted had abandoned us. We woke that morning to find all manner of chaos; he'd taken as much food as he could carry and the better of my two pith helmets.

I was despondent. Deep in a foreign jungle, without a guide and all manner of native bugs and insects and other sorts wandering about with any amount of infectious diseases. Spiders the size of your fist. Snakes so fearsome they'd sooner swallow you whole than look at you. Millipedes of the size and disposition of dyspeptic house cats. My own mortality felt imminent.

This is it, Mike, I said. We're going to die out here. This is the end of it, I'm sure.

He just smiled at me and put his hand on my shoulder.

We'll get through this, Bryan. We haven't had our last sight of the broad, majestic streets of Old Indy, yet.

Thanks, Mike. You're always the first to give your fellow man a reassuring pat on the shoulder, I said.

Actually, he said. I was killing a half dozen mosquitoes which were about to strike; I didn't want to alarm you.

He held up one of the offending gentlemen by the wing for my inspection.

This particular genus, he said, has an almost preternatural ability to spread malaria.

I nearly fainted — I've always been deathly afraid of the malaria; a great scourge upon humanity the malaria has been — but we soldiered on, he with his cool efficiency, me with my spare pith helmet.

Days passed. Our supplies ran low. We were down to our last can of milk. I swear to you Mike slept no more than fifteen minutes the entire time. Finally, just as I thought we'd hacked our machetes down so blunt they couldn't cut warm butter, I heard something.

Either the heat has gotten to me head and I'm hearing things, I said, or there's people nearby!

I tell you I near jumped out of my skin in excitement.

That's no auditory hallucination, Bryan. I suspect there is a village ahead.

He was right.

Things were no better when we stepped out of the jungle, however, for there stood a mass of angry locals and who was at the front of them, but Pasindu Ted, cock of the walk in my best pith helmet.

Pasindu Thedsanamoorthy, we mean you no harm! Mike called.

Ah, speak for yourself, Mike, but this piker left us for dead in the jungle, stole half our food and me pith helmet!

I fumed.

He shushed me.

Pasindu Ted said something to the crowd and they let up a mighty, angry roar.

What did he say to them, Michael? I asked.

He told them that we have come to steal the Red Hornet, he said. It's an ancient cultivar of chili so blisteringly hot few can tolerate the experience, and those who can are worshiped as minor deities. It is their livelihood. It is only grown in this region and is sold, blended down to reduce its potency but still retain its — I'm told, unmistakable —

character and then exported to markets the world over.

He stood tall and said loudly in Vedda, People of this village, we come in peace! We are not thieves or brigands, merely lost travelers.

I understand Pasindu Ted repeated his allegation.

This is a lie, good people. In fact I have never tasted a chili, much less one as renowned as the Red Hornet, valued the wide world over for its piquancy.

Now, that our friend Mike had never tasted a chili was true and I can vouch for it; he'd never tasted anything hotter than an old shoe.

The Red Hornet is your birthright, Mike continued. To steal your patrimony would be to steal your very souls. This would be a crime unspeakable. How may we prove our abundance of good will?

An ancient sage, leaning on a gnarled walking stick, came forward. The crowd quietened. Even the buzzing flies held their breath, waiting for the old man to speak, and when he did, it was in the low, measured tones of one who expects to be minded.

What did he say, Mike?

"Let the Hornet decide," he said and, looking me in the eyes, he repeated: Let the Hornet decide.

Even then no fear was in Mike's face nor voice. He strode confidently to face Pasindu Ted.

Now that face showed real fear. Sweat soaked his brow; he staggered back a pace.

The crowd parted and a woman bustled through with a basket overfull with little red peppers, each about the size of a golf ball. By local custom, Pasindu Ted, as the accuser, had to take the first bite, but right of first selection was given to Mike, as the accused. He reached to the basket and, with great decision, took his pepper. When the basket came to Pasindu Ted, however, his hand shook violently and he took great care to find the smallest one.

At the command of the old man, Pasindu Ted took the pepper into his mouth, and after a moment's hesitation, chewed. His agony was instant and terrible. He wailed, he spat the pulp out onto the ground, he clawed at his tongue, he vomited into my best pith helmet, then he reached for his eyes.

Careful around the eyes, man! Mike shouted as he jumped forward and restrained the tortured man's hands.

Here, Mike said. Drink this. It will soothe some of your pain.

And he handed Pasindu Ted the last of our canned milk.

Mike was not safe yet, for he still needed to withstand the Hornet's sting himself.

There he stood, before the people of the village, before the old man and the pepper lady, before poor Pasindu Ted. He put it in his mouth and chewed. And, no word of a lie, his omnipresent smile widened.

Why, golly, but that's got some zing to it! Mike said. And what a pleasant sweetness there is, as well. And, if I'm not mistaken, there's a dang delightful secondary heat coming. Yes! There it is! My, this pepper of yours is truly, truly wonderful!

The crowd cheered, men and women openly wept in the streets. Children were lifted onto shoulders so that they might for a moment spy the great man in their midst.

And — get this — he says to me, Bryan, you should try this!

Now, one look at your man writhing on the ground even after he drank the last of our milk and soiled my best pith helmet, and there was no way on God's green Earth I'd even consider allowing that pepper within arms reach of myself for even a second. But do you know what Mike did?

Well, I'll tell you what he did: He had another!

* * *

Sometime I'll have to tell you about the time I found myself in the middle of the straw hat riots.

30th May 2020

THE TIME MIKE TOOK ME TO THE GATHERING OF THE JUGGALOS

The following story is meant to be humorous, and is not intended to represent the real-life Mike Pence. As far as we know he did not, in fact, ever yell, "Titties!" at a group of scantily clad women.

Former Vice President Michael Pence has musical tastes for which the adjective eclectic is an understatement. I've known him man and boy and he still surprises me. Needless to say, his range of musical interests has led us down some strange, old town roads. I think you'll like this story; it's a good one, as they say.

It all started in his woody van, as it often does. A certain song was played in lieu of Pastor Dennis's latest sermon on the 8-track. I was disappointed as I'd been so looking forward to his sermon on chastity. He had an unfortunate vocal tic where he placed the emphasis on the second syllable rather than the first that I much enjoyed.

Michael, I said. How could you be listening to a character of the sort as this Neil Young?

I don't know what you're talking about, Bryan.

Well, I replied. How could you trust a man who rode his horse, alone, across a desert and never thought to name your man the horse? A horse is a great friend to Man. A coworker. A fellow traveler who endures the same class of hardships as his faithful rider or master. To deny the horse a name — what sort of a man does that?

Well, he chuckled. I don't know.

I'll tell you the sort: a no good ruffian of the lowest character. A vile cretin. The kind of man who'd befriend you on the trail and then steal your supper. A brigand. Perhaps even an Englishman.

Well, Bryan, he asked. What would you have named the horse?

Chuffy the Bastard, I replied, as quick as you please.

That seems rather harsh, Bryan, he chided.

Well, I can't imagine the sire and dam were married, now can I?

I suppose not, he said.

There was a silence, just the hum of the road and that damned "A Horse With No Name" on the 8-track.

Did you know, friend, he said. That this

song is often mistaken for the work of Neil Young but is, in fact, a recording by the folk-rock group America and written by one of its members, Dewey Bunnell.

Another uncomfortable conversational pause filled the woody.

Well, I said. I know my Helprin. *Freddy and Fredericka* is one of my favorite novels, of course. Anyhow, this song makes me feel dusty and dirty, like I've an exoskeleton of dried, flaky, odoriferous sweat.

He reached behind my seat and into a cooler and pulled out a bottle of the Faygo.

I think you need a shower, he said.

What the devil are you on about now, Michael? says I.

A Faygo shower is the cure for what ails you!

I don't follow, I said. I regarded him with deep suspicion.

You need to expand your musical horizons, Bryan, he said.

A dozen of the Faygo and several roadside micturation stops later we arrived at The Gathering of the Juggalos. I'd been given quite the musical education in the interim.

No, Michael, I said as we stepped out of Woody carrying all our kit. It's a perfectly reasonable question. You've got your positively charged gentlemen and your negatively charged gentlemen and between them a vast nothingness, as far as your men are concerned, being so tiny themselves. How do they, should we say, communicate, do you think? Is it all manner of shouting and the like and if so, what is the medium that carries all this attraction and repulsion information, as we've already established there's nothing there?

Bryan, he said with a broad smile. Don't you think you often overthink things?

I have extensive thoughts on that very subject, in fact, I retorted.

By then we were at the gate: tan lines and portable toilets the like of which you've never seen.

Now if anyone addresses us by shouting "Whoop whoop!" Mike said, the proper response is "Whomp whomp!"

I took out my makeshift Juggalo-English Dictionary and made entries for both Whoop whoop! and Whomp whomp!

We made our way inside. Never have I seen Michael in a place where ladies' breasts were more freely bared. A mere request and up went whatever served as a brassiere. He never requested it for himself, mind, but several times on my behalf he called for titties, covered his eyes and let me observe the display themof.

I won't call him a connoisseur but I cannot fault his curation.

Now, Michael, says I. What is your opinion of this Charlie whose cooking I hear spoken so well of?

He knows I have a great appreciation for the

culinary arts.

Bryan, says he. Our friend Charlie is not one who contributes to those, almost sacred, arts. He is instead a manufacturer of a powerful stimulant known as methamphetamine. He is otherwise a kindly soul, but his wares have ruined many a family and many a community.

Well, Michael, I said. You'd better believe they didn't teach us that sort of cuisine at Le Cordon Bleu.

I'm always ready to defend my Alma Mater.

At a stall Mike bought himself a spiderlegs hat with mock hair in that style. He resembled a Rastafarian who'd been struck by lightning. The sight of my great friend in that ludicrous hat — so prescient is Michael that he, in response to my soundless gaping and mad gesticulations, pointed out that famed Dirty South rapper Ludacris was not, in point of fact, performing at this gathering — was striking. It was like someone had painted Steely Dan into *Washington Crossing the Delaware.*

I must say my attitude changed over the course of that afternoon. There was a great sense of family and humanity to be found between the drunken wrestling bouts and the slasher references. Your man the Juggalo may not have a Harvard education but he can reassemble a diesel engine and give you a comprehensive explanation of the Cleveland Torso Murders simultaneously and with equal precision. An atmosphere of acceptance and commonality obtained throughout the event. It was a peon to the conciliatory nature of common interest and fellow-feeling.

It was beautiful to behold. I was taken up.

Michael, I said, filled with the liberality of the occasion. You should enter yourself in the Freestyle Rap Competition. I've no idea what that is, but it sounds like the class of event you might enjoy.

I swear to you, dear reader, I said that entirely in jest. I meant to spur no eccentricity nor reveal hitherto unspoken truths. I most certainly did not entertain the possibility that my idle question would result in the cataclysm that resulted.

You will be surprised to learn, Mike said. That I am forbidden from entering that competition.

Ah. Pastor Dennis, I replied with a laugh. A heretic, of course, but a stopped clock is right twice a day, they say, and twice a day he is.

No, you misunderstand me, says Mike. I am forbidden to compete in the Freestyle Rap Competition because I am a former champion.

I was flabbergasted. Your man engaging in a rap battle and claiming, over the course of several rounds of increasing difficulty, victory was a reality I could not imagine.

You, Michael Pence, I said. You blow smoke up my kilt. You've battled in no such manner, I'm sure. A strident argument? Of course. A witty rejoinder? To be sure. But all classes of this hipping and hopping? No such thing has ever happened, I'm sure of it. It never happened, or I'm not Bryan O'Nolan.

A quick visit to the registration table and I was sure that, come to find out, it had. A man that you know and that I know, Mr. Michael Pence, was a champion emeritus of that august competition.

Somehow in the confusion and bewilderment I'd been signed up myself.

Now Bryan, as a judge, he said — a judge! he says — I'll have to recuse myself whenever you're involved. The only exception is in the finals, when I will have no choice but to be a fair and honorable judge.

Michael, I said. They'll eat me alive!

No, Bryan, says he. They're fine fellows, and you've the gift of gab.

The finals were upon us before you could say, "Bryan how have you gotten yourself into such a predicament?" Never in my life have I been so nervous. I looked about me: A broad expanse of Juggalos: My new family, looking on expectantly, myself uneasy in the knowledge that no harsher judgment is rendered than that of family; my greatest friend the now-impartial judge of my hip-hop acumen; the rank smell of the marijuana and stale alcohol in the air. I knew that somewhere Shaggy 2 Dope was listening.

I was laid low by my opponent, a jolly brigand in torn bluejeans with a day-glo shock of hair in my favorite color, chartreuse, and a backpack that surely carried equal quantities of the Faygo and the methamphetamine. He called me a leprechaun. Something about St. Patrick and the snakes. He ended by rhyming "four-leaf clover" with "bend over". There was a grand ovation at this.

It was my turn at the microphone.

The mic was hot in my hands. The words crystallized in me consciousness as I felt the pocket of the rhythm. My mind was filled with the bevvy of rhymes I would bust and I rapped in the freest of styles. The last of these biting lines were:

> *Son you callin' me leprechaun*
> *An' I wonder how much meth you're on*
> *Here I'm doing calculus,*
> *You're tryna square the octagon*
> *I see you rapping*
> *With your lazy flow and mumbly voice*
> *Your rap is pants, son,*
> *I'm the freestyle James Joyce*
> *Your flow is whack,*
> *Your rhymes are iffy*
> *If you come into my neighborhood*
> *I'll toss you in the frickin' Liffey.*

Except I didn't say "frickin'."
Michael, I daresay, did not approve.
I lost.

* * *

Sometime I should tell you about the time Mike shot a Bald Eagle, which was critically endangered at the time.

2nd June 2020

THE TIME MIKE WENT ON AN AYAHUASCA-FUELED VISION QUEST

The following story is meant to be humorous, and is not intended to represent the real-life Mike Pence. As far as we know his face has never, in fact, turned into a liquid he could reach through to scratch the otherwise unreachable spot on his own back.

My great friend Mr. Michael Pence's great concern for the indigenous peoples of the world is well known. I've told tales of it before. Lesser known is how his worry about the fate of uncontacted tribes in the Amazon basin led to his voyage to the astral plane on an ayahuasca-fueled vision quest.

While Mike is a great supporter of

civilization as a rule, he is aware of the deleterious effects it can have on newly contacted tribal communities. As such, Mike made himself half of a two person delegation — myself, his unofficial Chief of Chief of Staff, being the other half in question — to Peru to consult with the policymakers and other local experts on the subject — from Members of State down to the shaman of neighboring tribes — very early on in his time as a Member of Congress. It was with this latter class of gentlemen that Mike, through a simple misunderstanding, found himself thinking about thinking about thinking.

We were meeting informally with one of the shaman in question when he asked Michael — in a manner both wily and duplicitous, as I recall it to mind now — if he would like to sample the local tea called Spirit Rope. Somehow through the Quechuan and the Spanish to the English the psychoactive nature of the tea in question was lost upon Mr. Michael Pence (R-Ind.).

He was told by your man the shaman to pick the lower leaf of the Chacruna at sunrise. I could see the Congressman's eyes light up. It was like we were back in our Dungeons and Dragons days and our Dungeonmaster Romney had given us a quest. A guide was hired, daysworth of provisions were acquired and — intrepid explorers we! — we trekked further into the bush accompanied by any number of well laden mules and manservants.

THE TIME MIKE WENT ON AN AYAH... 51

Forty-five minutes later we'd found the leaf in question and set up camp on the side of the highway to wait for sunrise. I confess at this point in the adventure I had no idea my great friend would be purging the contents of his digestive system as a prelude to inter-dimensional travel within the next eighteen hours; I just thought it was an overly complicated attempt at a good breakfast tea.

In the early morning I awoke to the sound of scraping, or so I imagined.

When I came to the campfire — mere embers now, if even that — there he was: shirtless, sharpening his machete like its next victim was to be a holy blood sacrifice to appease an angry goddess and sweat glistening in the sunlight off his chest like he was some toned, damned demigod himself. I wondered what Richards would have thought in that moment.

Mike spoke without even acknowledging my presence.

Has the sun broken the horizon yet, friend?

Not yet, as far as I can tell, said I.

The lower leaf of the Chacruna will be cut this morn, he said. Or I'm a Masschussettsan.

A soft rain fell upon the broad leaves of the jungle; somewhere birds took flight, calling in the twilight. The last scent of smoke from the campfire married the earthy smell of the jungle and filled my nostrils.

Is that the proper nomenclature for a

person from the Bay State? I asked.

He worked the whetstone up and down the blade of the machete methodically.

It is, he said, after a pause.

Somewhere a howler monkey, well, howled. As they do.

New England is a very strange place, I gather. Are your men from Connecticut—

Connecticutians, he intoned.

Well, that's just absurd, I said.

Indeed, He said without altering the rhythm of his sharpening, his eyes on the blade, always. So is Connecticut.

No truer word has been spoken in my hearing. I knew our dialogue had rolled into its terminus and I'd need to disembark. I wandered off in search of breakfast. I recalled there being many a rasher of bacon and they called to me.

Instead I heard a primal scream, a great, guttural yawp.

All of your men the manservants awoke.

I ran back through the bush: great leaves and branches were tossed aside as I ran willy-nilly, to find the gathered masses about our friend Congressman Michael Pence, he having cut the lower leaf of the Chacruna. The dawn was just then breaking. When I arrived he held the leaf high and a hushed silence obtained about the assembled observers.

I have, he said, as one who who speaks great words aloud that echo most deeply in his own soul, opened the great double doors of the dawn.

What do we do now Michael?

His eyes met mine. He looked like he had only just realized the rest of us were there, like he'd just snapped out of a dream.

Why, Bryan, he said, clapping me on the shoulder, we take it back to our good friend the shaman, and we try this tea of his.

Within an hour we were back at this shaman's village and walking into his hut. My eyes stung from the smoky air. Mike and I took our place at the benches.

What other ingredients constitute this fine tea? said Mike as he watched the brew boil over the wood fire.

Oh, various indigenous vines and shrubs, said your man the shaman.

I watched him with a shady eye, I did.

Did you say vines? I said. Michael, are you really going to subject yourself to this? I was hoping to learn a few new things about my good friend the potato while in South America, but a tea made from vines? And did I hear your man say something about shrubs? This isn't the class of shrubs you were getting for the garden from that Roger fellow back home, I'm sure.

The shaman kept it at the boil and added Mike's leaf with a flourish. I thought this was a theatrical bit like the onion volcano at a hibachi restaurant but our friend Michael was by this point completely engrossed in the show of it.

Yes, Bryan, he said. I expect to enjoy this tea.

Your man the shaman was at this for hours. I thrice nearly fell asleep.

At a moment which seemed as unimportant as any other, the shaman stood and said, It is time.

A draft was pulled and handed to Michael. One was offered to me but I declined with a glare of steel,

Alright, Michael, I said. Down the hatch. I feel like the longer we stay the stranger this place will get.

No, Bryan, he said. I mean to nurse this cup. I want to know the subtle contours of this tea and explore the depth of its flavor. I'd think you'd want to join me, given your culinary expertise.

He drank. He rolled it around on his palate. He wafted its bouquet. He eyed the ceiling in concentration and when it was done he, despite my strenuous protestations to the contrary, accepted the shaman's invitation to stay and chat.

Half an hour later Mike stood suddenly.

Excuse me, he said. But I need to use the jungle.

He ran out, myself right after him.

Michael, I said. What is it?

Fire drill, he said. Everybody out by the nearest exit.

And right there he dropped his pants and engaged in simultaneous vomiting and diarrhea, both of the projectile class. No more pathetic sight have I witnessed in my life. I daresay the monkeys looked impressed, though.

This, proclaimed the shaman from the door of the hut, is called the Purge. It is a cleansing force.

Cleansing? I asked. Cleansing? Certainly not to the poor trees. You mean to suggest this is a feature? "Come to my restaurant; you'll be spouting bile and liquefied feces from their respective orifices!" It's a wonder the restaurant scene is as quiet as it is around here! I said, sarcasm dripping from my tongue like the contents of Michael's digestive and excretory systems dripped of the nearby jungle flora.

Bryan, Mike said.

I looked at him.

He had a thousand yard stare and stupid grin upon his countenance.

Why is a Bottom called a Bottom when it is more generally in the middle?

I rounded on your man the shaman.

What have you done to Michael? What is this Spirit Rope?

Come to find out our friend had just embarked on a vision quest, facilitated by your man the psychedelic chef, courtesy of a witch's brew called the Ayahuasca.

Suddenly Mike burst out in laughter and said to a tree with which he imagined himself conversant, One, two, three! I've ears enough to hear you!

He stared, listening.

The forest buzzed.

Then I may sleep in spite of thunder, he said. Sweet bodements! Good!

Let's at least get you cleaned up, Michael, I said. I helped him, as only a best friend can.

Once he was cleaned up and re-pantsed we began to take him back into the hut. However, before we could get there he looked at me, shock covering his face.

Bryan, he said, I don't mean to alarm you, but your face is melting,

I decided it was best to play along.

Do you tell me so, Michael?

Lucky for you, I know just the remedy. Hold your face in place as best you can, I'll only be a moment! And off he ran to a stand of beautiful flowers and, after careful selection, he used his drawn machete to cut one and brought it to me.

This will solve the problem, he said. It is lucky for you that our souls have been entwined outside of time as brothers. Otherwise this cure would not be efficacious.

I nodded dumbly and put it through a button hole of my tweed jacket.

He looked uncomfortable, but reached over his shoulder and scratched his back. What was most remarkable was that he looked amazed as he did it.

What is it, Michael?

You didn't see? he asked as if I'd neglected

to realize we were in the jungle, so blind was I. My head is become a liquid such that I can reach through it to scratch my own back! Even the unreachable spot!

We took him back into the hut. For a time he was quiet and sullen. He put his head in his hands.

I was almost afraid to ask.

Mike, I said. What is it?

He looked at me like a child who'd lost a puppy.

I am a string, Bryan, he said, of infinite length, plucked.

He shed a single tear.

Now, Michael, says I. I'd think that'd be a good thing, being a soul that sings and all that.

He cheered immediately. His smile spread across his face and filled the smoky hut.

Bryan, he said with a smile. I knew you weren't really an ape.

Eh? How's that?

Well, apes almost never wear a hat.

Several hours — and halfway between Lima and our changeover in Houston — Mike was no longer convinced he was being stored in the overhead luggage compartment.

Sometime I should tell you about the time Mike prevented a shark from beheading a moose.

6th June 2020

WHATEVER BECAME OF DORA THE EXPLORER?

The following story is meant to be humorous, and is not intended to represent beloved children's characters living or dead.

The stars that burn brightest often burn out the soonest. Whenever people wonder whatever happened to that beloved star of yesteryear, Bryan O'Nolan investigates.

It was a quiet Tuesday at the Ordinary Times Investigative Bureau, Building Three, Third Floor. The sunlight came through my Venetian blinds at just the right angle to make the shadows and the flickering light on my desk suggest an air of mystery and a hint of, shall we say, things best left unsaid. Stones best left unturned. I had my feet up on the desk and a pipe was being contemplatively smoked by myself when the telephone rang.

The call came from one Alicia Márquez.

Make it quick, Ma'am. I've little time, I lied.

I want you to find my estranged sister, said she. She was famous once.

I knew the routine: brought joy to children; had her own show; probably a toy line, if I'm not mistaken.

I was not mistaken, of course.

Our family has broken apart, she said, We, no, I — I don't know if they do — regret the fame, the notoriety, the licensing deals. We didn't know where the money would go. We only knew there was money. It tore us apart.

To be sure, to be sure, I said. But who is the sister?

She was known professionally as Dora the Explorer.

Well, sure and I'll tell you I couldn't believe it. I was very familiar with her work, having managed her fan club for several years, but I'd moved on to other things. To hear that she'd disappeared and that she, Alicia and Diego were all estranged from each other was quite a shock. Quite a shock, I tell you.

I know where Diego lives, Alicia said. But we're not on speaking terms.

That's all a hard-boiled gumshoe like myself needs: a lead. I was on my way to his exotic animal park in central Oklahoma that afternoon.

Diego! I shouted, stepping out of my dusty

rental car. I have to speak to you.

What in the hell do you want? he said.

He was quite confrontational.

I was wondering if you had any information regarding the whereabouts of your cousin Dora García Márquez, I asked.

How did you find me? Was it that bitch Alicia Márquez? He said, poking a finger into my chest. He smelled of cheap cologne and what I assume was tiger musk.

I decided the equivocation was my only reasonable play.

Well, said I. It was a complicated flight with stops at both the Heathrow and the Dallas Fort Worth before getting into the Will Rogers. Then I rented the very Chevy Cavalier you see behind me now and —

So you're not from New York?

I am not, I said. I am familiar with that fair metropolis in reputation only.

He eyed me suspiciously, but it appeared Diego was not the sharpest tool in the junk drawer.

Look, if I help you, she can't find out, because if she does — back to the chest-poking now — I will never financially recover from this.

I merely nodded in agreement.

Talk to The Map.

Luckily for me, Map could easily be found in a Tulsa dive bar, smoking a cigarillo and drinking lite beer for breakfast; he was a broken Map.

I ordered a southwestern-style omelette

and orange juices from the hungover barkeep. I can't stand the small portions of orange juice doled out by your men the restaurants.

No backpack? I asked jovially, hoping to soften him up.

Map just stared at me for a moment.

You really thought there was a talking backpack?

Well, I'd just assumed—

That was CGI. You know nothing about show business, pal. Nothing, he spat. They tell you you've got a future. "There are plenty of parts for a singing map!" they say. They said there's growth potential. Maybe someday I could play an Atlas, or a singing Gazetteer! They don't pay you scale for the better part of two decades and tease that you have a future for your own benefit. You need to know how the game is played. Now Blue: she played the game right; got the right contract and had the good fortune to be a dog. Everybody loves dogs! Nobody loves maps.

I love maps, I said.

I knew if I could keep your man talking I might get somewhere.

This ain't that kind of place, hombre.

An uncomfortable silence obtained in the bar. My omelet arrived.

So how did this Blue do so well? I asked.

The underdone omelet slid down my gullet like a glob of warm mucus with an admixture of raw pepper and onion chunks. It tasted no better.

Luck and good representation, Map said, lighting another cigarillo. Same old story. And boy, did she make bank. I hear she's down in New Mexico, somewhere. Still working, the bitch.

Do you tell me so? I said as I sipped my orange juice.

Yeah, he said, as he took a long, sardonic draw on his cigarillo. Still working. Look, Blue broke up friendships like it was going out of style.

You don't say! I said.

I mean we were competitors. Same network, but there was a serious rivalry between the two productions. The Nickelodeon back lot was a tough neighborhood in those days. Can't tell you how many times Mailbox would sneak onto our set and yell, "Freeze, Bobos!" just to ruin a perfect take. I had to bail Boots out more than once — out of my own damn pocket, you understand — when he'd get caught messing with their sets and equipment. One time he changed one of Steve's cue-cards to say 'I love cocaine'!

The Map smiled and shook his head.

Boots was the worst criminal I've ever met. There's no plan he'd undertake — let's move on to the gin course, Shirley — that he didn't get caught on account of his own stupidity. Somehow he never did any time.

Map stared down the ash on the end of his cigarillo.

I've heard it said, many a time, I offered. That people that dumb are already in their own sort of prison. Do you follow?

He was getting choked up.

Still, the dumb bastard didn't deserve what he got in the end.

He was crying now.

I'm so sorry, I didn't mean—

I threw an arm around him.

He took a moment and just cried. He wept in my arms, the poor map.

Look, fella, he said as he regained his composure. When someone tells you there's more than one way to steal a threshing machine you spit in his damn eye for Boots 'n me.

It was quite a pronouncement.

Ah, I think It'd be best to change the subject, don't you think, said I.

Thank you, friend, said Map.

You mentioned Blue and a divisive friendship? I dipped a conversational toe in ever so carefully.

Now, you didn't hear this from me, Blue and — he looked furtively round the bar before mouthing "Dora" — were friends. She betrayed the whole cast! We'd worked so damn hard to stand together and the whole time she and Blue were palling around and none of us knew. We were humiliated.

As it turns out, Map, said I, that Dora is the very person I am trying to track down!

He took a napkin and wrote down an address. It was in New Mexico.

Word of warning, friend, Map said, with a look of disgust. You're going to want to call first. Somebody might need to fit you into her busy schedule.

He rolled his eyes and returned to his drink. I left a fifty on the bar with a nod to Shirley indicating it was for your man the Map and — do you know? — when I left the bar I thought I heard him humming a happy, mappy old tune to himself as the bittersweet memories washed over him.

I'd just got to the airport when, out of nowhere, a bipedal fox — oh, I immediately recognized that dastardly Swiper! — took the napkin out of my hand.

Dear reader, excuse me for being so direct but we are at an impasse. If you are unable to yell, "Swiper, no swiping!" three times at the text of this story then I will be rendered completely incapable of finishing it, leaving you in a state of unresolvable suspense for which I could never forgive myself. Can you do it reader, for all of us? Wherever you are, yell it — "Swiper, no swiping!" — now!

Ah!

Oh, thank you, readers. Please express the sincerest of my apologies to your fellow passengers, members of the clergy and any other witnesses. If they look at you questioningly simply tap the text with a knowing eye and say, "Ordinary Times" as if that were all the explanation any reasonable person could need.

We may now move on.

The New Mexico. They say it's a dry heat. But to those of us from the rarefied airs of the higher latitudes, a dry heat is still damned uncomfortable. I wanted climate control and an interview with this Blue; she wasn't the only one who could follow clues.

Forty-five minutes after claiming she couldn't fit me in until Tuesday next she suddenly had an opening in her busy, busy schedule. Something about two projects in development and feigned regret at going into directing.

I was there in half an hour; she had the climate control I required.

I'm so happy you could fit me in, I said, taking out a notebook the size of which implied I had a much greater interest in all she had to say than I actually had. While you are, perhaps, most known for your breakout work in *Blue's Clues*, I know you've been ever so busy since then. Could you tell me more about that?

I was taking the soft approach, you understand.

She lounged on a memory foam doggie bed and chewed briefly at her fore-paws.

I am, of course, she said. Very proud of the work I did on *Blue's Clues* — I think we made an important difference in many children's lives with that project and broke a lot of new ground — but I'm just as proud of my more character-driven work.

Ah, said I. Do you tell me so?

Well, so they say, she said with patently false modesty. One doesn't appear in the first three seasons of *A Game of Thrones* on good looks alone, does one? That's where the real work is done. The constant interplay between oneself, the other players and the demands of the production... well, let me say that is where real art is being made, these days.

I knew I had her; she was waxing philosophical, which is where you want a person with no philosophy to be when you stick the poignard in.

Skilled with the rapier as I was, I held off for the moment and took another line of attack.

Do I hear you played Buck in the recent production of *Call of the Wild*? I said lightly.

She groaned and stretched in her dog bed. An assistant brought an ice cube and placed it in a dish full of water.

Loved working with Harrison Ford, she said. Consummate gentleman. The script was a shambles, though. I stuck it out for the sake of the project; to do otherwise would be unprofessional. To be in a production of London, I mean, could any canine actor want for more? But making the narrative focus a human was wrong and I opposed it to no avail. You win some, you lose some in Hollywood. As long as I win some? I'm happy.

I wonder what role affected you most deeply?

Oh, playing the title role in the West End production of *Old Yeller*. Lin-Manuel Miranda is an absolute genius and, unlike most geniuses of my acquaintance, an absolute delight to work with.

Now, Blue, I said. As much as I respect your storied career, I have another question to ask you. You were very close to one Dora the Explorer. Have you any notion at all of where she might be at this time?

She became serious: this was a Blue I'd not yet met or known.

If what I hear is true, she said, trailing off. She wrote an address down on a card. It's an arena in Mexicali. You'll find her there, I think.

As I thanked her and excused myself I think I saw Blue go over to her dish and — delicately, mind! — take the ice cube out of your man the water dish and over to one of your gentlemen the carpets.

Now, I don't have any Spanish, so it was several hours later through all sorts of gesticulating on my part and manys a knowing glance between your men my escorts, I arrived at the area in question.

This was not a high end affair. On the floor of the arena there were no chairs. In the center was the ring. There were four *luchadoras* in and around it in their striking and garish masks. I gathered the ladies were having a tag team match.

It would make sense that a person known for working in front of the camera might transition to artist representation and management when their more public career dried up, so even though Mexican Wrestling was an odd choice of field, it would at least explain her near complete disappearance.

The crowd let up a roar at something in the ring, but I wasn't watching that. I was wandering through the crowd towards the scorers' table in hopes that the managers and agents would be nearby.

Just when I'd got to the cordon that kept the fans from the ring there was a loud clang and a sudden silence. I looked to the ring and one of the wrestlers was holding a metal folding chair in the air and standing over her prone, unconscious victim. The victim's partner stepped into the ring.

You have broken *kayfabe*! she yelled. You have injured my friend.

And that's when it hit me: Her voice. I had just laid eyes on the target of my search: Luchadora the Explorer. I rushed to the edge of the ring as some medics pulled the bleeding, unconscious wrestler to the floor.

Dora stepped toward the attacker, veins pulsing in her massive muscles. She was angry, I could tell — I knew she and her show so well — but she didn't look angry. She never did.

The attacker swung the chair; Dora ducked and took the full brunt of the blow to her back. She hit the mat hard; we ended up face to face.

You are Bryan! she said. I signed a t-shirt for

you once. I remember all of my friends!

She reached out to me. I touched her hand.

I'd been tagged in.

I took off my shirt, put on elbow pads and climbed to the topmost turnbuckle.

You'll regret that, or my name's not Bryan O'Nolan! I shouted.

I leapt off the turnbuckle and had the one with the chair down on the mat in a rear-naked choke hold in a flash.

Welcome to the jungle! I shouted as she struggled for breath.

Her partner jumped into the ring. Dora was on her as quick as you like and just as my opponent passed out, Dora had hers up in the air for a Backbreaker. She brought the girl down on her knee and let her roll onto the mat.

I stood up.

And now, I said to the whole arena. Here comes my finisher!

I took off one of my elbow pads and tossed it to an eager fan in the front rows. I swung my arm dramatically across my chest and bounced off the nearby ropes and ran full tilt across the mat — with a skip over the body of my target — a great lean into the ropes beyond and then, when I had ricocheted off that and was back at my enemy, I lifted my leg and delivered, mercilessly, The Peoples Elbow, right to her breast bone.

Dora came over, took off her mask and we raised our hands high in victory.

We did it! We shouted in unison.

* * *

Sometime I'll have to tell you where Waldo was all that time.

13th June 2020

THE TIME MIKE KILLED AN ENDANGERED BALD EAGLE

The following story is meant to be humorous, and is not intended to represent the real-life Mike Pence. As far as we know he has never, in fact, dressed as a woman. Not that there's anything wrong with that.

To tell you the story of the time Michael Pence shot the endangered bald eagle is a funny enough tale, worthwhile in its own right — it's a good one, I think you'll agree — but it's also an opportunity to tell you about a great friend of mine, Booper McCarthy, may the poor fool rest in peace. He died as he lived, a great, lovable, gregarious imbecile. But that's another story.

This one begins on a cold Monday morning some January or another. Mike and I belonged for many festive years of blessed memory to a

Morris Dancing side that specialized in a particular tradition called the Molly Dance. Every Plough Monday — first Monday after the Feast of the Epiphany — we'd march down to the village and perform our program for the village folk. Bells about the ankles, the auld songs that Grandad used to sing, good, strong cider for the tall and soft cider for the small. Mike played the part of the Molly for our side, which required him to dress in glorious, ostentatious drag and specially adorned combat boots.

I'll come back to that bit in a moment, of course.

As we were preparing to head out we came to a moment of crisis. You should understand, now: My great friend Booper and I had the role of the pantomime horse. I was the front, as no person in their right mind would let McCarthy drive. That he was the horse's arse was not lost upon anyone who knew him. What was, in point of fact, lost by all of us that clear January morning was one Booper McCarthy.

Bryan, Mike said, I'll check the girls' dormitories down by the nursing school. I need not tell you of the intensity of his interest in the fairer sex. You check the woods hereabout.

So check the wood I did. It's a wild, primordial forest, bounded on one side by the village and the other by a broad river. It was not long before I'd met the fool in the forest. The motley fool. A miserable world! As I do live by food

I met the fool wandering through the wood.

Now, Booper McCarthy, I said. You know we've a dance today and sure and but it's starting soon!

Bryan! says he, taking his watch-and-chain out of his pocket and holding it lazily up to his ear. Ah! Don't you know I'd forgotten to wind the blessed thing!

Never mind the dial, I said. Whatever the time it is, you're late for the show.

And just like that, I dragged him off to our staging area.

I'd managed to get the two of us dressed in our halves of the costume. Performing as a pantomime horse requires the intuition and skill one would usually associate with the nuance of the ice dancer. As one partner moves so, too, must the other anticipate and accentuate the other. It is a delicate and subtle conversation of motion. There are few finer arts than these, in truth, the ice dancing and the pantomime horse.

McCarthy, said I, what rhymes with "purple" and what, I asked catechism-fashion, does it denote?

The answer to your question, Bryan, said Booper, and an impertinent question it is, is "curple" and it means the backside of a horse or donkey.

So it does, said I. He grabbed my belt and we, together, became a horse. I'll not say that we made the best of horses, but the village judge, one Dr.

Martin Dysart, gave us rave reviews. We pranced and danced and reared for all and sundry. Children laughed and tugged at my ears and the tail on McCarthy's bum. It was a great show.

Meanwhile Mike made merry in his pretty pink polythene floral dress and Doc Martens, the latter of which he'd adorned with rainbow and unicorn stickers. Spins and suggestive poses the like of you've never seen. One minute he's a brazen Jezebel and the next he's the village Pollyanna, skipping about and collecting daisies. Much laughter was had at his broad antics.

His dancing involved a shotgun.

I should probably explain the shotgun.

Many Morris Dances involve some class of prop derived from or imitating a weapon, be it a play sword or a dummy long gun or, in some traditions, a broomstick. Mike preferred to do his Molly Dance with a no nonsense break-action double-barreled shotgun. Beautiful gun. Always in the best repair. Treated it like a wife, he did. Little did we know that he always had a pair of slugs stored in his brassiere.

We'd just assumed—

Excuse me.

Now, at any rate, we found out that weekend that there were to be explosions from the business end of these guns.

We went to bed tired men that night. We fell asleep still dressed in our costumes. Or, at least, most of us slept. Booper, despite his obstructed view as a horse's ass, had apparently scouted the co-ed population with a remarkable thoroughness.

It was when I woke the next morning that I realized he was again missing. Michael was roused and the search was afoot. We decided to invert our previous search strategy. Michael was to the wood; I to the nursing school.

When I got there the sun was just breaking over the rooftops. The village was still asleep. There was a drain pipe which leaned away from a corner of the dormitory like it was offended by the building's presence. I saw the handiwork of one Booper McCarthy in that saddened drain.

I was soon inside the building and awakening all its residents with a spoon and a pot lid like a town crier at Pompeii. I have no idea where the spoon and pot lid came from. It turns out it was all unnecessary, of course, because when I glanced out a common room window I saw your man walking down the street with a puppy in his arms.

I barely made it out of the dormitory alive.

Booper! I called once I'd caught up with him at a park by the river.

He turned and with that broad grin of his he greeted me.

I hailed him with the standard Irish greeting.

Níl fo-éadaí á chaitheamh agam!
And he gave me the typical response.
Is fraochÚn í do mháthair!

It is always a blessing and a joy to hear the great and melodious sound of the Irish spoken!

Now, Booper, I said, out of breath, what do you mean staying out at all hours? And where in the hell did you find a puppy?

To the former, he said, I will merely confirm your suspicion that I met a bird. To the latter I confess absolute drunken ignorance; but he's cute and I've named him Dalkey.

Sure and don't you think your bird or whoever is going to want him back?

He looked genuinely perplexed.

You might be right; you might be right, said he, thoughtfully.

And your man the flaccid drainpipe beyant, I take that to be your work as well?

He responded only with a smile that was equal parts pride in having attempted it and relief in having survived the attempt.

Well, we need to find the owner before this turns into a reported case of the petnapping. I have heretofore kept your preposterous decision making out of the papers and the courts and I'll not lose my clean sheet over your man Dalkey, as cute as he may be.

We headed back towards the nursing college: past the peddler who inexplicably sold chipmunks and squirrels in cages, past the purveyor of strips of fabric; past the tennis ball seller and the peddler of things that squeaked when you squeezed them; past the poulterer's and past the butcher's.

Now, Booper, I whispered conspiratorially. We don't want to arouse any suspicion. Let us skulk round this corner and see what we can see.

We stuck our faces round the corner and were immediately faced with the double-barrels of Mr. Michael Pence's shotgun.

Unhand the puppy, nefarious brigands! he shouted.

Booper instinctively dropped the puppy in question.

Michael, it's just Booper and me! I cried, as Dalkey ran off in the direction of the butcher's.

Egads, man! Mike said, lowering the gun and putting a hand on my shoulder. If only I'd known, I'd have been less confrontational. But our friend the pup is away: We must pursue the lad until he can be brought to ground. Make haste.

Haste was made and we were off in the direction of the butcher's but our hopes were dashed when the handsome mutt saw us and decided to run off with a marrow bone the size of his head to explore the poulterer's.

We were gaining, though.

Just as Booper pounced on him, Dalkey snuck through his grasp and headed toward the High Street where the peddler who sold things that squeaked when you squeezed them — an idiosyncratic feature of the Molly Dances in our village he was, and a delight to the local dog community, if a nuisance to their owners — over the traffic-polished cobbles he went like a terror to the squeaking.

We carefully crept up to the stall, each of us trying not to make any sound, each of us mindful of any movement, you know.

We've got him surrounded! I shouted, but at the same moment a tube of tennis balls was upset at the stall beyond and the balls bounced down the hill and Dalkey was off like a flash, right between my legs and chasing the Penns and Wilsons down the High Street.

Mike had a moment of blessed intuition.

To the seller of fabric samples! he cried. This Dalkey looks like the sort of lad who'd like to pare down a strip of furred cloth as fine as he could make it. Perhaps we'll find him thus distracted!

We were off again, Mike with his gun, me with my wits and Booper as, I suppose, what you might call moral support.

Merrymakers filled the streets with noise and confusion.

Mike's intuition was right, of course, for there we found Dalkey, happily tearing strips of fleece with his mouth and fore-paws.

We crept up as silently as we could; Mike had his shotgun drawn.

Dalkey worried the strip of fabric mercilessly. He was singularly focused on the process of tearing the large bit into smaller bits.

Through the employment of grand gestures we espoused a plan wherein Mike would flush him and Booper and myself would tackle your man the dog. Had the plan actually been carried out, I suspect the result would have been several concussions but this was not to be, thankfully as Dalkey saw us as we moved in and he escaped us at a run towards the Chipmunk and Squirrel Emporium.

I should at this point mention that, at the time this story took place, your men the Bald Eagles were critically endangered. They have recovered to a great extent in many parts of the United States, but it is important to recognize that, when this story occurred, your men the birds were very much in the neighborhood of the extinction. A sorry state, a very sorry state they were in.

Some drunken fellows in the crowd toppled over the cages of your man the Vermin Peddler Supreme. His wares were scattered across the cobbles of the village square. Dalkey had a bead on a chipmunk of ill repute and was after him at speed into the wood.

That's when it happened: a beautiful, strong, Bald Eagle swooped in and grabbed Dalkey in his talons. Mike didn't hesitate but, taking a slug out of his bra, loaded it and shot the eagle as it took flight. Dalkey fell a foot or two to the ground and, shuddering, was taken back to his person, who renamed him Michael, after the hero who had brought him home safe and sound and none the worse for wear.

* * *

Sometime I should tell you about the time Mike attempted to take his family from Independence, Missouri to Oregon's Willamette Valley in a covered wagon having only supplied them with wagon axles and ammunition.

19th June 2020

THE TIME THAT MIKE ENCOUNTERED A WENDIGO & I INTRODUCED HIM TO THE FUTURE MRS. MICHAEL PENCE

The following story is meant to be humorous, and is not intended to represent the real-life Mike Pence. As far as we know has not, in fact, nearly soiled himself in the Maine Wilderness.

Most people don't know that I was the person who introduced Mike Pence to the future Mrs. Michael Pence, but it's true. Not only is it true, it's a snorter of a tale into the bargain as well. It's about the time he met not only the love of his life, but a creature — wrongly assumed by many to be mythical — in a part of northern Maine known in that fair state as The County.

I briefly ran a kitchen after my graduation from Le Cordon Bleu. This endeavor I abandoned after a harsh review entitled "No-TAY-tow, No-TAH-tow". It was a blow below the belt, to be sure — what we call an Irish Uppercut — but I know when I'm told. I can take it just as well as I can give it out; no shame in that.

But the whole affair got me thinking about the reviewing business. It all boils down, if you understand, to "Is it good?" If I'm to move into the assessment business, I'll need to find myself in the market where people most want assessment.

"Did you have a good day?" is a question I imagine to be more frequently asked than any other, with the exception of "Why?" If a question is asked so frequently, I figured, there ought to be some remuneration in providing an answer. I decided to go into the Day Assessment business. Follow a person about all day and at the end tell them whether or not they had a good day.

I enlisted the help of my good friend Booper McCarthy, put up a shingle and started the important business of business, that is, ordering office supplies: pens with "How was your day? Ask Bryan O'Nolan!" embossed on the shaft; letterhead; pre-printed envelopes in all sizes. I tried to order commemorative bobbleheads of Booper but the disproportionate enormity of his great head caused them to topple over.

Meanwhile, we had no clients.

Bryan, Booper said, what if we did some work on what you call the speculation?

Whatever do you mean by that, Booper McCarthy? I said. The speculation.

My da, when he was just going into the building and such, erected a building on the speculation, under the theory that your men would walk by and, impressed by his erection, want a building put up for themselves.

Booper, I said. Your da was a fruit-seller.

Well, that's because he wasn't very good at the maintenance of his erections, but the theory is there all the same.

I see what you're after, I see it now.

It would be the last time I would take advice from one Booper McCarthy, *requiem æternam dona ei, Domine*, the blessed fool.

We resolved to follow people around for a day at the end of which we would provide a thoughtful and incisive review. We would track and record every movement made, meal taken and conversation held.

It turns out this is considered "stalking" in

several jurisdictions.

After posting bail we were despondent. If the speculation would not get our business going, what would?

I was pondering this very question when into my office walked a beautiful woman with dirty blonde hair and the clearest blue eyes you ever saw this side of Galway. I'll just say that it was lucky that Booper was marching up and down the high street wearing a sandwich board advertisement at that very moment.

She was unsure of what service my business provided. I explained it as best I could. I offered her a 100% discount, and she accepted.

Let me tell you her next day was a wonderful one. The zoo. Lunch at an up-and-coming sandwich shop. Museum in the afternoon. Supper at the hipster place no hipster would countenance in six months. A five star day.

How did you plan so wonderful a day? I asked.

Well, she said, I'm on vacation.

And what do you do for work? I asked.

I run an outfitter in Aroostook County, Maine, that specializes in canoe trips through the wilderness down the Allagash River.

She was the only client Booper and I ever had.

So it was that the following October, Michael and I were in her shop — and he in her thrall — purchasing supplies for our adventure.

And what an adventure it was!

We employed a pair of guides for our trip, a French Canadian fellow called Défago and his partner of twenty years, Hank Davis. The former seemed somewhat reticent to accept our business — skittish, you might say — but he relented.

Into the humming wilderness we paddled our canoes. I with Défago and Michael with Hank; the future Mrs. Michael Pence was our last sight of civilization and she promised she'd be our first when we'd got to our destination.

The first few days were relatively uneventful.

Moose and bear were plentiful, as were Hank's tales of hunting and trapping. Even more plentiful were the black flies, a horrid little creature that breeds in running water and feeds on people. One would think that pure, undiluted DEET would keep the bastards at bay but you'd be wrong in that assumption. The DEET does nothing in that regard but it turns out it will erase the print off your t-shirt. Meanwhile your men the black flies buzz about unbothered and feast happily on any available human flesh.

So, bug-netted and begloved we paddled the Allagash waterway. At one point Hank and the more taciturn Défago held us up so that we could make the rapids at the precise time when we wouldn't have our canoes swallowed by the whitewater.

It was on the evening of the third day that

things began to go sideways, as it were. We'd pulled up our canoes to make camp near an abandoned lumber train — engine and cars just left where they were, made the more beautiful by their dereliction; it was as if they were being reclaimed by the forest itself — we slung our food in roped bags over high branches against the Old Brown Man of the Wood, Honey-eater, the Shaggy One. We'd seen him and his sort on what you might call the periphery watching us like the very eyes of the forest primordial itself.

As we made our tent, Défago turned to me and spoke. It was a rarity that he spoke not in answer to a question.

Mr. O'Nolan, he said. Do you smell anything... strange?

I put my able nose to the air; nothing but the now familiar mixture of forest smells and DEET did I find there, and I told him so.

Ah, good! It was nothing, then, he said, though I did not believe he was as relieved as he wanted me to think he was.

I needed a talk with Michael, and forthwith.

He and Hank were encamped some ways away, but I marched right over and pulled himself away from the fire to speak in privacy.

Michael, I said. Have you noticed anything queer about your man Davis? This evening Défago has been in a right state and, I tell you, I don't know what to make of it.

No, Bryan, he said. I've noticed nothing out

of sorts. He appears to be his usual gregarious self. I've offered to teach them my favorite card bluffing game, Bologna Sandwich.

I was getting all anxious myself.

Michael, you don't think they're cannibals or stray carnival folk or something like that?

Mike just laughed.

No, no, Bryan, I'm sure they are not. But I'll be sure to keep a weather-eye on Hank, though, if that will ease your mind.

I thanked him and returned to the bit of the camp laid out for Défago and me.

Défago was still looking nervous. He was the quiet sort, yes, and tried to keep people at arm's length, yes, but I'd taken a shine to the man, don't you know. He was good, honest folk; I felt a brotherly care for him.

Défago, said I. There's something bothering you, there has been since before we even embarked. What is it, man?

Have you ever heard of the Wendigo? here he laughed to himself. Of course you have not. They say there is a devil which inhabits these cold northern forests. He hunts for men. And there is a — how do you say? — characteristic scent before he strikes. It is, they say, both sweet and repulsive at the same time. Just as you arrived I heard from a fellow guide — an indigenous person native to this land, you understand; not like you or me — that the Wendigo was on the hunt. He had smelled it.

He kicked our fire; little did I know we were

borne into trouble, as the sparks flied upwards.

He laughed another feeble laugh.

It is nothing, of course, he said.

We retired to our cots.

I was soon asleep, though I daresay Défago was not.

I woke in the night to his wordless fussing. He was not sobbing: no. But he, in his sleep, was clearly in some emotional distress. I was greatly saddened for the man, though there appeared to be nothing I could do to soothe him.

Then I smelled it: an acrid sweetness. I can only say it smelled like death.

There came a sound, like a great torrential river of wind, crashing through the forest that stopped at our tent door.

Défago sat up, his eyes wide like saucers. Suddenly his cot was dragged by no earthly force I could name to the doorway and he sprung out of it and ran into the forest. I followed as best I could once my wits were about me but I'd lost him almost instantly.

I went and roused Michael and Hank.

When I'd finished sputtering my story and gesturing incoherently Mike's face bore a look like he might soil himself at any moment. On Hank's was a look of terror.

Why, we must, Mike fumbled. Organize a search.

Don't bother, Friend, Hank said.

Whyever not?

Hank fixed his gaze on me.

Did he tell you about the Wendigo?

I recounted what I knew.

Well, mister, Hank spat defiantly into the fire. That ain't the half of it. Ain't by a long stretch.

He pulled some jerky from a small packet he always carried and worried it in his mouth.

The Wendigo is a cruel devil that feeds on human flesh. A starving giant. Every time the bastard feeds he grows as much as he ate, so he can never be satisfied.

And I thought, Mike said. That the witch in Snow White was the most frightening thing I could imagine. Jiminy creepers!

It's a damn terror to look on, they say, Hank said and spat again. It smells like death, and it looks like a giant, haggard, emaciated victim of its own rapacious hunger.

We were silent for a moment.

Mike made a low whistle.

Well, I'll be gosh darned to H-E Casey Kasem, he said.

Would anybody mind, I suggested, trying not to sound as terrified as I was. If I just grabbed my things and joined the two of you for the night?

It was agreed; but even once situated, none dared sleep, nor even enter the tent. Hank sat, back to the fire, watching the forest. Mike and I were on tenterhooks.

Michael, I whispered, for I wanted none but he to hear my voice. Are we to be eaten tonight by this vile creature? I daresay I never thought I'd go as food. A cautionary tale, perhaps, but never as food.

Gird your loins, Bryan, said he. Tonight may be a hard one.

Don't bring my loins into this, Michael, I retorted in whispered indignation. The only feast my mortal remains will be for is worms! To suggest I become rubbed and marinated cuts is unspeakable. I won't have you describing me as delicious.

You'll note, friend, he said. That I did not speak of that possibility. Cleave your worries as close to reality as you can and we'll make it out okay.

I put my Earthly faith in Michael as I always have. If he says we'll make it out alive, then I'll believe it until it's proven false.

As happens, he and I both dozed off in our watching.

It came upon us in a flash: a mad cacophony of wind and fury and sound that scoured the descending forests about the wild river and stopped before our camp. It breathed heavily before us. It inhaled us and knew the innocents who lay before it.

We, all, turned ourselves to the menace: It huffed and it breathed its foul, hellish breath.

Up it stood, a great presence from without the world-henge. Emaciated, its skin stretched across its bones, a shape half like a man and half like a starved wolf. But in the features of its face there was an unmistakable likeness to —

Défago? Hank creaked.

The beast's nostrils smoked.

Dé-fa-go! it growled. Dé-fa-go!

Please don't eat him, Mike said, nodding his head in my direction. He's Irish.

And then, as suddenly as it had come, The Wendigo's face folded in disgust, it turned and ran off into the forest.

We made the end of our trip in record time. And, as promised, was the future Mrs. Michael Pence waiting for us. Three paler men she could not hope to meet.

*** * ***

Sometime I'll have to tell you about the time Mike got kicked out of the Emergency Room for flipping off everyone in it.

27th June 2020

THE TIME MIKE FOILED A JESUIT CONSPIRACY TO INFILTRATE & SEIZE NEW BRUNSWICK

The following story is meant to be humorous, and is not intended to represent the real-life Mike Pence. As far as we know he is not, in fact, an expert in 19th century whaling techniques.

Part The First

Of the youthful summers that live sweetened by time and memory in my mind, the summer my great friend Mike

Pence and I, along with and our friend Romney, spent as lighthouse keepers in Downeast, Maine, may be the sweetest. Little River Light, on an island at the mouth of the Little River in Cutler, Maine, played host to one of the most spectacular incidents — which is also one of the most closely kept secrets — in Mike's life. At least so far.

This tale is about an event one cold, haily, windy night that opened our eyes to the world around us and — I don't want to overstate the matter, mind — made for a quick and unceremonious death of innocence for the each of us. A bildungsroman, if you will, with stress on the dung.

That summer, Pence, Romney and I took over as temporary keepers of the light, through some class of arrangement concocted by Romney's father. The usual keeper, at that time one Humphrey Chimpden Earwicker, had jury duty and was hearing a case against the Lubec Police.

The short white lighthouse and the rustic, homely keeper's house we found there — do you know I can still smell it when it is called to mind? — was home to honest work and earnest laughter.

To live on an island is to live on a flake of the sea so tempered by the cooling face of the waters that it is become a slowed sheaf of the fragile earth. Our little island was, facing that disconsolate sea, all great blocks of rock piled against each other haphazard like with a lone, short promontory. But atop those rocks were green grass, pine trees and an abundance of guano, which Romney collected in buckets.

One day I saw him plant an enormous flag of his own creation — a great Roman R gules, on a field argent — in the middle of his favorite guano patch.

Romney, I said as Mike and I approached him, Explain yourself.

He swung his arm to encompass the vasty fields of guano.

What do you see here, gentlemen?

Rocks, said Michael.

And what upon those rocks, friends?

Bird shit, I answered.

Droppings, Bryan, a great fortune in bird droppings, Romney said. And I propose — no, declare — that under the authority granted to us as United States citizens by the Guano Islands act of 1856 this Island, abandoned at our arrival, is hereby claimed for the United States and I declare, also, that we three are it's governing Triumvirate. Welcome to Romneyville, gentlemen!

Romney, it wasn't abandoned, I replied. You are a mad — I was lost for an apt geographical descriptor for him.

I wonder, Michael, I said, turning to him. Is he a Massachusettsan, a Michigander or a Utahn?

I'm a citizen of this island, friend, Romney said. And so are we all.

He clapped me on the shoulder.

Michael, I said, it's a stupid new world that

has such creatures in it.

I left it to Michael to talk some sense into him and went back to the keeper's house to check on my chowder. I could hear, through the open kitchen window, Michael patiently trying to explain the Missouri Compromise.

By the time supper came round Romney had accepted that you can't just go around staking a claim to any bit of poop-covered rock you find and our conversation on that eventful evening circled around the order of watches for the night.

Romney, as was his wont, began the conversation at the end and left it to us to work out how we'd got there.

Now, I want to, first of all, acknowledge the fine, fine job Mr. Michael Pence did last night spelling me for forty-five minutes while I overslept my watch. He is a good man and worthy of the respect and admiration of the American people. It is thus with great pleasure that I nominate a man of no lesser stature, a humble man who I think all will regard as worthy of the post, the gentleman from Howth Castle and environs, Mr. Bryan O'Nolan, as the leader of our night watch. Mr. President I do now formally nominate Mr. O'Nolan as keeper of the first watch, he said.

But, Romney, I cried, you've not been on time for a single watch the entire time we've been here! Nor have you had first watch on any evening in living memory. Michael, I have a low opinion of this—

Now, Bryan, I can understand how you feel, Mike interrupted; he always did this whenever I was likely to step in it. While I agree that Romney has not been holding up his end of the bargain, I suspect — here a meaningful glare was made in Romney's direction — that a schedule could be made that all will adhere to.

Well, sure and it's fine but your man over there needs to hold up his end of the bargain.

Bryan, Mike said, I think we can have a more substantive discussion over breakfast.

And so it was that I took the first watch on that fateful night.

The others were well abed when I made my way to the light to check the oil. Dark, it was, and unseasonably cold. A storm had drawn in with the night. The wind drove me toward the lighthouse like the meanest taskmaster of old Egypt, short way though it was. Inside the lighthouse itself the sound of it was even worse. The brick and steel structure was like a fun-house climbing up it, all the howling and the gusting and allsorts circling upwards and the thunder echoing in the tower.

At the top, standing about our fifth order Fresnel Lens and looking seaward, hail lashed my face, rain soaked my jacket. But I thought I heard something else amongst the sea noise and wind. Something like wood breaking and smashing, crying voices. As the light passed over them I could see two men floundering in the offing, clinging to a bit of the remains of a broken wooden dinghy.

Sometimes one's life feels like a great Rube Goldberg machine of infinite complexity and that one is merely the kinetic energy moving through it. I have never felt this more literally than I did in my attempt to get down the lighthouse's spiral stair.

I slipped on the first step and rolled, arse over teakettle, the entire way to the bottom. I think I counted enough bruises the next morning to account for each individual stair.

At the bottom I stood, dazed.

I vomited.

I collected myself.

I sounded the alarum bell. There'd been a wrack! I needed rescue harness on my back.

Mike was roused and moving by the time I'd got to the house. I quickly explained the situation. We gathered our gear and headed to the rocks. In the surf we found a man clamoring up, a great confusion of smashed lumber and, treading water, a great fat skellig of a man, his face white with cold and panic, being pulled back out to sea.

To the rescue boat, Bryan! Mike yelled. I think I know a way we can rescue our enormous new friend!

We got the rescue boat — a longish inflatable character — and a ponderous length of rope and had the boat in the water in no time. I was at the oars and Mike stood in the bow, like your man George Washington, but tying what looked like a great noose. How could even Michael save the man? I wondered.

What in the hell are we doing, Michael? I shouted over my shoulder and the ruckus of the storm.

I gather you're unfamiliar with my treatise on the modern rescue applications of 19th century whaling techniques, friend.

I am indeed, I am indeed. What do you mean to do with the rope? I can't imagine you want to hang the poor man.

He laughed to spite the wind.

No, Bryan! he yelled. No, I aim to lasso him. I just hope he doesn't take us on a Nantucket Sleighride!

Oh, that was the last thing I'd need, the great fella diving deep and trying to take us with him.

Sleighs are just fine by me, but I once met a man from the Grey Lady — the tales about him are greatly exaggerated — who I wouldn't trust driving a screw, and the Nantucket Sleighride is one of my great fears, one of my few greatest fears.

Mike called out directions and I used my — I flatter myself to say, rather well-developed — rowing skills honed on our remarkable trip down the Allagash River, to maneuver the craft within range.

Mike had tied himself a lasso big enough to capture quite a large person.

He swung it in widening circles above

his head. Lightning cracked above our heads. At precisely the right moment he loosed the lasso and it carried out through the wind and landed atop the waves with your man the large at its center. Mike girdled him up and between my rowing and our friend's feeble attempts at swimming the three of us were ashore.

We met the large man's compatriot and we stood in the grass, collecting our breath. The castaways wore yellow parkas like fish stick salesmen.

I'm Shem and this is Shaun, one of them said. I confess, dear reader I could never establish with any certainty which was your man Rosencrantz and which Guildenstern.

How do we find you here, friends? Mike asked.

They shared a sidelong glance.

Well, the svelter one said. We've heard wonderful things about the New Brunswick coast.

The what in the hell now? I interrupted. You're not in New Brunswick, you're in Maine.

Just then Romney appeared, yawning in his alarmingly brief bathrobe as he strode down the stairs.

Well, dadgumit, Romney said with a smile, Here comes everybody!

That was when Mike grabbed my arm.

Bryan, he said with deep suspicion in his voice. Our guests' voluminous parkas are concealing Roman collars! There's something going on here, or I'm not Michael Aristophanes Pence!

Something indeed!

20th July 2020

THE TIME MIKE FOILED A JESUIT CONSPIRACY TO INFILTRATE & SEIZE NEW BRUNSWICK

The following story is meant to be humorous, and is not intended to represent the real-life Mike Pence. As far as we know he did not, in fact, foil a Jesuit conspiracy.

In part one, Mike, Bryan and Romney were spending a summer keeping a lighthouse, as the regular keeper had jury duty. On a dark and stormy night, two men were shipwrecked on the Island. Upon closer inspection, it was discovered that they were priests.

The Thrilling Conclusion

It took all three of us to get the big one before the fire.

Once our visitors, Fathers Shem and Shaun, were drying — their great yellow raincoats hung by the fire — and had had a few glasses of water, the interrogation began.

Saints alive, I said. What were you two lads doing in the waters at this time of night?

Your men looked cagey.

Glances were exchanged between them.

We were, Shem said. Hoping to find some lobsters!

They were met with the combined silence of ourselves: Michael, Romney and me.

We were told that Maine was Vacationland and were hoping to explore its vast, beautiful wilderness? Shaun suggested.

But, wait! Michael interjected. Outside earlier, during the first part of this strange incident — you know, it almost feels as distant as last Saturday — you said you thought this was New Brunswick.

There was a great, uneasy silence.

Alright, Shem said with a sigh, We're Jesuits.

Careful, friends, Romney said, stepping in, still wearing his indecently brief robe. I have heard of these fellows. I suggest that we exercise an abundance of caution in our diplomatic relations. It's my understanding that they work for the Vatican and represent a secretive and pernicious sect, a mystery even to the faithful of their religion.

Well, I wouldn't say sect— Mike began.

Michael, I interrupted. You might not be the man best placed to speak on the issue at hand, given your, shall we say—

I prefer "faith journey."

—faith journey, thank you, I said; I rounded on your men the Jesuits. Now you two listen to me. As the representative bead teller and Friday Fish Fry partaker on this glorious island I want the two of you to understand something. By Clement the Fourteenth you'll give us the straight dope and the God's honest unequivocated truth and if we don't get it you'll find yourselves suppressed into the North Atlantic faster than you can say *Dominus ac Redemptor Noster*. Secondly, though of no less importance: I know me Catechism back to front and there'll be no heresy on my watch.

But we— Shaun began.

Are Jesuits, and let us leave it at that. I turned to Mike. They're all yours.

But wait, Shem said. Is there an order you *would* prefer?

The Dominicans, I said without hesitation. Many's the Saint with the OP after his name. A nobler and a holier order than the Greyfriars you could not find.

That's true of many orders, including ours; why the Dominicans?

I put the knuckles of my clenched fists heavily on the coffee table.

I don't see any Albigensians around, do you?

Shaun turned to Shem and Shem turned to Shaun.

I have to admit he's got us there.

Michael, I said, have at them.

Thank you, Bryan, Mike said to me. He clasped his hands behind his back like a country lawyer of days gone by, like your man Atticus Finch himself — nobody could be Gregory Pecker than Michel at his most lawyerly — and turned his attention to the soggy fellows on the couch.

Thank you for your eventual honesty on the question of who you are. But I ask, friends, why are you here, stranded and soaked to the skin on the bold coast of Maine?

We were hoping to evangelize— began Shem.

I cleared me throat.

We were trying to sneak into New Brunswick, Shaun admitted.

I don't understand. What reason could you possibly have to infiltrate our kind neighbors the *Néo-Brunswickoises*?

They eyed me, cautious.

Why did you have to sneak in? Mike asked

with frustration in his voice.

How else were we supposed to get in? Shaun said.

Passports.

They turned on each other.

You told me that wouldn't work! Shem said.

The Superior General told me to prepare as if it might end at Mount Unzen, I didn't think we could just, you know, walk in!

Real vitriol between them in the air, now.

I spent two weeks hidden in a shipping container full of raw cuttlefish and we could have just waltzed into Fredericton? I am having very uncharitable thoughts about you right now, Father.

At least you didn't have to consort with grave robbers and get smuggled into Tangiers in a sarcophagus you shared with one of the Pharaoh Inyotef II's lesser wives, Father!

Mike cleared his throat.

It seems, he said. That you gentlemen have gone to extreme lengths to get here.

Do you want to tell him about what happened to the sled dogs, or should I?

There was finger pointing into the bargain now.

No one told me not to give them chocolate macadamia nut cookies!

We were 30 miles outside of Kwethluk in January, that's no time for questionable doggie treats!

At least you still have most of your toes!

That's not the point and you know it!

Gentlemen, gentlemen, Mike said, quietening them. Let's just stipulate that you went through a monumental effort to end up here.

They shuffled until they could be no farther apart and still be said to occupy the same couch, each with defiant, folded arms. They glared pointedly away from each other. It was then that I began to understand Mike's prosecutorial strategy. He'd managed to divide them and had pitted them against each other. From now on, I suspected the information would be flowing more freely, out of fear that the one would incriminate the other.

Gentlemen, Mike began. The established facts so far are these. You, firstly, have, at great effort and expense, sought illegal entry into New Brunswick. Do you disagree?

No, sir, said Shem.

Secondly, he continued. This evening you, to the uncouth end aforesaid, have been dishonest in your dealings with us, your rescuers. Do I characterize this aright?

Yes, sir, said Shaun.

We, your rescuers, Mike said. Given the facts stipulated to just now, have reason to suspect your intentions. Are we wrong to do so?

No, sir, Shem again.

One of you, Mike was laying out his case, methodical. I don't know if it was Father Shem or Father Shaun who uttered it, suggested that your destination was the capital of New Brunswick, Fredericton. Do you deny it?

No, sir, it was your man Shaun this time.

What were your intentions once you'd arrived in that fair city?

The two of them eyed me, fear in their countenances. My eyes were as cold as the Arctic frost. They were silent.

Michael, I said, I'm no canon lawyer, but I suspect we may be seeing the equivalent of the pleading of the fifth amendment in their silence.

Hm, Mike said and pulled me into a sidebar discussion in the kitchen. What do you suggest?

Well, it seems to me, I said, if one source of evidence has dried up, perhaps we should pursue another.

What do you mean?

We search their belongings, I said. Cast a wider net for new evidence. If they will not betray themselves, we let their belongings do it for them.

I'd the auld twinkle in the eye then. There was no way — no way! — your men the Jesuits didn't have incriminating documentation upon themselves.

Romney! Mike called to him from the kitchen. Search them. It is long overdue.

There was a scuffle in the other room but when Michael and I reentered order had been restored.

I found nothing more incriminating than this, Romney said, tossing over a copy of Mao's

Little Red Book.

It is not, I spat, uncommon to find upon a cleric a copy of his holy text.

But, friends, Mike said, we have searched the men themselves. But has our search been thorough enough?

He turned his eye to the fire, about which hung the great, yellow raincoats your men the Jesuits had worn.

Romney, Mike said, the raincoats!

There was a brief fracas as Romney pounced upon the raincoats in question and the Jesuits dove haphazardly and, ultimately ineffectually, toward the fireplace. Romney then stood, victorious, with a sheaf of paper ensconced within a zip-top bag.

He tossed it to Michael.

The Jesuits re-arranged themselves on the couch, now looking more cowed.

Michael opened the bag and took out the document it contained.

"For your eyes only," he read. "A Plan To Establish The Holy Roman Empire Of Canada"?

What is this about? Mike demanded. Out with it!

Shem let out a great sigh.

We were sent to infiltrate the government of New Brunswick with an eye to turning it into a Jesuit enclave.

He sank into the couch.

Ave Maris Stella! I shouted. You can't be

serious, man. This is an international incident we have on our hands, here.

Bryan, Mike said. Bind them. We have a few phone calls to make.

A few hours later some *federales* from an agency unknown to ourselves had taken them off our hands quietly and, luckily for us, it was on Romney's watch. First one he'd made on time that summer. He was never late again.

You'll be pleased to know that Father Shem is now a most holy chaplain at a federal prison in New York and Father Shaun is now a Dominican Friar well known for his piety, *laudete Jesus*. Or was it the other way round?

❊ ❊ ❊

Sometime I'll have to tell you about the time Mike met his Progressive neighbors. Actually there's no story there; they don't discuss politics when they socialize and, in fact, Annie makes the best ziti and Pam is more than happy to look after the Pence family's pets whenever they vacation.

22nd July 2020

THE TIME MIKE SQUANDERED THREE WISHES GRANTED BY A CRONE

The following story is meant to be humorous, and is not intended to represent the real-life Mike Pence. As far as we know he can not, in fact, whistle loudly without using his fingers.

My great friend Michael Pence has many admirable qualities, but patience and thoughtfulness when granted three wishes by an old crone in a German forest is not among them. It's a great story — as unfortunate as it is — so unfasten the topmost button of your pants and prepare for a belly-buster!

It all began on a tour of small-town America, as it so often does. I have little memory of what town we were in, but the ample meat display I will remember and cherish to my last breath.

Bryan, Mike said as we studied the counter resplendent with meats and cheeses, I've always held that you can best judge a town by its delicatessen; and you can best judge a delicatessen by its selection of that undisputed king of cold cuts, ham.

Do you tell me so, Michael?

I do indeed, he said with a confident smile.

But what if it's a kosher or halal delicatessen, what then?

Why, then let the corned beef be your guide, Bryan!

And what, I asked, in theory, would one do if one found oneself — due to the beautifully variegated quilt that is American culture — in a delicatessen owned and operated by a half-Jewish, half-Hindu couple? What then, Michael?

The kosher dill pickle will never steer you wrong, my friend, he said.

So true, it was, and I told him so. Never a Lithuanian Half-Sour have I had that I would not use as a culinary lodestone.

Let's take a tour of the hams, shall we, Bryan?

I looked hungrily at the rows of hams, hams of every shape and flavor. So rapt was I that Mike needed to get my attention with a friendly tap on the arm. He held a canned ham before him.

What is your assessment of this selection?

Well, I said and took a breath to steady my nerves, ensconced in a disgusting jelly, it is best thought of as a food to stave off starvation or as improvised ordinance for use in a catapult or trebuchet.

I see your education at Le Cordon Bleu taught you well, he said. Let's take a look at the more palatable options, shall we? Here we have a honey ham. It advertises that it is made with Wildflower Honey, but that's just clever marketing.

Naturally, I said, calling it Wildflower Honey is just another way of saying you've no idea what your men the bees were fed on.

Exactly, said he. Here we have a Virginia Ham — also known as a Country Ham — of which the people of the great state of Virginia are understandably quite proud. Salty, smokey. A delight on any sandwich it may encounter.

That is, I said, tasting a sample, a fine ham.

Here, he said. Taste this. A fine Italian Prosciutto. From Parma, I believe.

It was delightful, and I told him so.

We are missing, of course, the Spanish *Jamón*, I said.

Not so much a cold cut to my mind, more an appetizing *tapa*, I think you'd agree? Mike said. Allow me to introduce to you the Black Forest Ham.

Well, I said, chewing. This is an absolute delight.

Here the man behind the counter got Mike's attention with a conspiratorial wink and nod.

Sir, he said, glancing to ensure that we were the only meat-seekers privy to the discussion. Have you ever had Black Forest Ham that came from the actual Black Forest region of Germany?

We shook our heads and were soon led through a series of locked doors into a meat cooler in the Employees Only area of the delicatessen. He showed us a ham on a proud table.

What do you detect? the deli hand asked.

Your palate is superior to mine, Bryan, Mike said. Training tells.

I whafted and whiffed and snoffted and sniffed the ham carefully. I closed my eyes and chewed, immersing myself in the expansive universe of flavor provided by your man the ham.

Garlic there is, especially, I suggested. Black pepper — no, no it's Indian Long Pepper! — and coriander, too, or I'm an Italian. But I do think there is a lovely embrace of the juniper. There: I said it. How did I do, *garçon*?

Parfait! the deli-hand declared.

Bryan! Mike ejaculated, chewing the meat. I had no idea that the Black Forest Hams of Germany had such intricacy, such an expressive depth of flavor!

Needless to say, we were bound for the Baden-Württemberg region of Germany forthwith.

Before you could say, "*Wie sind wir hierher*

gekommen?" we found ourselves deep in the harsh, heavily forested borderlands of old upon the South German Scarplands looking out upon the plain of the Upper Rhine.

We — he dressed to the nines like a Swiss hiker, myself in my usual Harris Tweeds — traced an ever-fading track into the darkest part of the wood. Shadows waved menacingly. I swear I could hear the howl of the wolf and the tread of the bear in the forest all about me.

I saw something on the ground.

Michael, I said. It looks like there's a pile of goldfish crackers on the ground. Whatever do you think it means?

I've heard tales of children leaving themselves a trail they can retrace as they head into some dangerous, fell wood. A wood such as this. And see here! he said, pointing to a continuing line of crackers along the path. A trail, like Theseus's thread!

Theseus, said I. Was something of an asshole, if I'm to be honest.

Nevertheless, Bryan, I think we may be following such a track.

We followed the trail deeper into the wood. Trees creeped upon us; owls cried. I was encouraged when the trail went from the cheddar flavored goldfish crackers to the inarguably superior Parmesan expression.

What, I asked in speculation, do you think we shall find at the end of this trail of woe,

Michael?

Likely, he said, a crone who tempts children into the deep forest only to throw them into an oven, or so I'm told.

Eventually, we came to the edge of a clearing, with a hovel at its center. The goldfish crackers had thinned out long ago; I had hoped they'd led back to civilization by tired children.

I knocked on the stout oaken door.

It happened in a flash: the door opened, a face appeared and Mike had reached in and grabbed the threadbare woolen hood belonging to the face, dragging it into the clearing.

It was a crone, indeed. She eyed us suspiciously.

Well, gentlemen, she said, her voice like a creaky door, I suppose I'll have to be granting ye three wishes.

Is that each, I asked. Or all together?

Sadly for you, matey, they all go to your friend here who actually captured me, she said, poking me in the chest with a laugh. Standard Genie Rules apply, of course.

Mike let go of her hood.

She was flippant, I thought; I immediately wondered if the rules were hard and fast, or up to the granter. I still don't have a firm answer to that question.

Wellsir, Mike said with a laugh. I feel completely unprepared. I supposed I'd like a sandwich — no, make that *two* delicious sandwiches, one for my friend here — made from that delightful ham native to these forests.

Her eyes widened, questioningly, but she made no comment. A man who thought so infrequently of his own wants was bound to foul up an opportunity such as this.

Granted! she shouted.

A brown paper bag appeared before us.

I worry about your instincts here, Michael, I said.

Do you dispute that a sandwich made by another is superior to a sandwich made by oneself?

Well, no, I said. That is an immutable law of nature.

I confirmed the contents of the brown bag.

Would you believe she was thoughtful enough to include napkins and your men the little packets of the mustard and the mayo, Michael? I said. But be sure to let me advise you on the next of your wishes.

Haha! No, Bryan, said he. I know of just the thing for my second wish. But, crone, I want to know that you understand exactly what I'm talking about here. You know how some people can whistle very loudly by using two fingers in their mouth.

Of course, she said, confusedly.

Do you know how some people can whistle the same bright, clear tone by just breathing over their contorted tongue?

Yes.

That ability is my wish!

To whistle loudly.

In just the manner described, yes.

She sighed.

Granted!

Satan's woolly socks, Michael, I said. This won't do, you've squandered away two perfectly good wishes and I won't let you do the same to a third.

Now stop right there, boyo, the crone said. You haven't tried the sandwich yet.

Michael let out a piercing whistle.

Well I'll be a monkey's uncle, and if need be, sturdy father figure or mentor, Mike mused, mostly to himself. But isn't that the sweetest, cleanest whistle you ever heard?

Yes, I said, entirely devoid of spittle, Michael. Now you listen here—

That's enough of your Now Listen Here-ing, Mister, the crone interjected. You leave the man to his last wish.

I folded my arms in indignation and leaned against a tree.

Mike scratched his chin, ruminating upon this vital, final choice. A bird chattered in the tree above. I briefly considered that its pooping on my head might be the most fitting end to this misadventure.

Mike nodded in satisfaction; an idea had come upon him.

I assume I can't wish that you'd give up on trying to lure children to your hovel in order to bake them into pies?

Nope, sorry, hombre, she said. When you've got a brand, you stick to your brand.

Then I'd like a cool and refreshing sweet tea.

Saints preserve us, Michael! I shouted.

And then it hit me, warm and goopy down the back of my neck and into my shirt: I'd been shat upon.

In fairness to the crone, the sandwich was delicious.

The sweet tea was excellent as well.

❋ ❋ ❋

Sometime I should tell you about the time argued in court the difference between a pond and a lake.

1st August 2020

THE TIME MIKE PREVENTED A SHARK FROM BEHEADING A MOOSE

The following story is meant to be humorous, and is not intended to represent the real-life Mike Pence. As far as we know he could, in fact, use his fingers to count to ten, were it necessary.

As striking as it sounds, Michael Pence did indeed once prevent a moose from being beheaded by a shark. Pull up a chair by the fire; it's a tale for the ages. This took place while Congress was in recess, so Mike was free to join our friend Hoff and me in visiting Richards on Cape Cod.

Richards is a great one for the surfing. So often were the times we watched such classics as *The Endless Summer* and *Crystal Voyager* at university that Michael and I developed a great love of the surf music, in point of fact we formed a band of that sort, but that takes us into other stories not of this moment. No, it would be no surprise to those who know him then that Richards would bring himself to the crashing of the waves and the surf as often as was humanly possible.

Thus, that fateful visit, we found ourselves out at just the tip of Cape Cod. A more beautiful example of the insignificance of the land in the face of the sea you could not ask for: to the north lay the well whale-grazed upland of the Stellwagen Bank; to the south stood the slender forearm of the Cape herself; to the west was the pleasant, eddying bowl of the Gulf of Maine; to the east, the unpacifiable Atlantic herself, all winds and ice-floes and the old sea chanties.

I'm in great awe of the sea. With a ship beneath me I'd've gone to her man and boy, but I do not, you understand, consider a surfboard to be a ship, by any measure. So when Hoff and Michael and Richards were out at the surfing I stayed ashore, surreptitiously assessing the skills of your men the lady lifeguards. I take a great interest in the public safety, don't you know. Who watches the watchers? Why, Bryan O'Nolan himself, that's who!

I also took a great interest in the local population of Grey Seals. I'm a great man for seals and otters and allsorts. Such personality they have! Your men the seals were quite about, this day; very playful, almost cantankerous.

The scream I heard froze everyone at the beach. There was a scurry in the water and a geyser of blood and before I knew it, Mike was before me with the tip of his right middle finger spraying blood like Bernini's *Fontana del Tritone* in the Piazza Barberini in Rome.

Shecking Alefridonk! Mike moaned, wordlessly.

There was no hope of finding the missing bit so we wrapped the wound up as best we could and bore him to my car, the last eighth of his count to ten lost among the waves.

But where was Richards? Come to find out he'd commandeered a sand-castle builder's shovel and was angrily cudgelling to death your man the tiger shark that'd done it.

Richards! I cried. We've got to take your man Michael to the hospital!

He gave the bastard a kick in the head and was in the driver's seat in a flash. I'm little use in a crisis most of the time and besides, he knew what you call the lay of the land much better than I. We careened down highway and byway, swerving in and out of traffic, Richards waving to the policemen who all seemed to know and think well of him. In point of fact, before long we had a police escort.

Richards, said I in wonder, I've never met

a man who was so well known to the local law enforcement who was also so clearly well liked. I am very impressed.

He merely smiled, the story behind which he would evidently never tell.

We arrived at the Emergency Department of the nearest hospital and were immediately shown into a room. Richards was in a panic.

Now, Micahel, I said, be sure to keep it elevated above your heart.

And, Mike— Richards exclaimed.

Stop with the shouting, Richards. Saints preserve us! I muttered.

Mike, Richards said, emotional but at least he'd stopped yelling. I don't want you to get any blood on that beautiful Hawaiian shirt. Hold your hand out at arm's length.

At that very moment the physician's assistant entered the room.

What seems to be the — she was stunned into silence by the sight of Michael, spinning to face her with his right middle finger projected at arm's length from him and directed at herself.

Fnock mnoff, Mike sputtered, waves of pain crashing on his personal shore.

Sir! This is rude and inappropriate, she said.

Mother! he called for the Missus in his delirium. Fugger.

That's it, the nurse fumed and turned and left the room, the door slamming behind her.

I could tell by the look on his face that

Richards was scanning his fertile mind for a solution. But before he could find one, the Chief Medical Officer — said so on his name tag, so it did — strode into the room. Before he could even speak, Michael, uncouth finger thrust before him, was moaning again.

Snabvavich, he cried and then he cried.

You, sir, The stern medical officer said. Will restrain yourself or you will have to be sedated or removed from this department.

Bryan! Richards said. I think I have a solution.

Before I could enter into even preliminary discussions with him Michael made the issue moot.

Kizmmass! Kizmmass! He shouted and the whole department turned to us in horror.

Moments later we were back in my Reliant Robin Estate and Richards was driving like a madman through the streets.

Dick, I shouted, where in the hell are we going?

He used the hand brake to make a sharp turn at a stoplight in what you call a Massachusetts Hockey Stop.

My seamstress, he said, cool as you like.

Well, long story short a week later Mike was bandaged and recuperating nicely on Richard's love seat.

Richards, he said. I'm thinking I need to understand these creatures, sharks. Despite — or, perhaps, because of — my recent experience, I suspect that they may be grossly misunderstood. There may be relevant legislation—

At that point the telephone rang. I answered the same. It was Booper, calling from our Investigative Headquarters. A great mystery had been reported. Beheaded moose had been found! Just the thing to distract Michael from your men the sharks.

Michael, I said. I'll brook no argument on the matter. You're coming with me to Lubec, Maine and you're to help me in an investigation. It's just what the doctor ordered.

He knew not to argue with me so lickity-split we'd chartered a sailing ship and Richards had found a crew. Hoff would captain us up there across the Gulf of Maine himself. Richards would make arrangements for my car. Right renaissance men Hoff and Richards are.

In the lower forty-eight you can not find a township east of Lubec. It sits on the great Passamaquoddy Bay, an inlet of the Bay of Fundy, the great engine of the Gulf of Maine: vast tidal exchanges, reversing falls and whirlpools. A short span from Lubec and you're in New Brunswick on Campobello Island. The Canadian White House. Franklin-bedam-Roosevelt's summer holiday spot. Gorgeous place; wonderful people thereabouts.

We pulled into a quiet dock just after the bridge.

Your man the Complainant was there with

a contractor to help with the investigation — a friend of Booper's, I gathered — a man of few words known to us only as Doug Who Works Under Water. We met in a parking lot hard by the waterfront.

Mike asked if he could take over as lead on this investigation; I happily obliged.

Alright, fellows, Mike said. What's the case?

Well, the Complainant, a State Game Warden, said, we've had a number of unexplained beheadings in our moose population lately. They're localized here, and the bodies are always found in the water.

That would, I suppose, Mike said, explain the presence of our new friend Doug Who Works Underwater.

Honestly, I can't say, said the Warden. That was mere intuition on the part of Mr. McCarthy.

I see. Mike was taking extensive notes.

Have you, I ventured, found any of the *captibus* about?

The what? the warden said.

Heads. Have you found any of the heads and if so, where?

Mike eyed me and gave a nod of respect, I being the more experienced investigator, of course.

Nope, he replied. Nothing. That's the real mystery of it, you see. Poachers will often take the head, but they'll take meat as well. And dumping what they don't want in the water? Well, that doesn't make a damn bit of sense. Not only is poaching a crime but so is letting a game animal go to waste. Now, I don't mean to step on any toes, but it looks to me we've got a killer here who just wants to kill for sport. Sickening.

Mike strode over to Doug Who Works Underwater and clapped a hand on his shoulder.

Now, he said. Mr. Doug Who Works Underwater, we need you to investigate these crime scenes to see what we can glean from them, as much of a fool's errand as that may seem. Any clue, no matter how small, would be a boon.

Doug Who Works Underwater nodded and we all boarded a ferry commandeered for the exercise. He and the Warden — the former by gestures and the latter in words and pointing — settled on and directed the captain to the most likely spot for investigation, a relatively shallow spot — we could see the seaweeds and kelps growing up from the channel floor — and there we set anchor. Mr. Doug Who Works Underwater prepared himself and was over the side before you could say Doug Who Works Underwater.

Tense minutes passed and we saw nothing of your man below. An osprey circled in the blue air above. It took off with a fish — face to front, each by each — and flew to shore. Cormorants plied the surface, hunting for themselves.

Suddenly there was a frothing of the water and there hard by the boat was your man Doug Who Works Under Water with a great shark in his arms. They went under again and, by the time they'd surfaced again, the Complainant had his gun out and shot the beast. Blood stained the water, but Doug Who Works Under It and the shark floated to the surface, the latter lifeless.

We heaved the bastard shark onto the deck. Doug Who Works Underwater made a scissors gesture.

Rock! I shouted, pounding a fist against an open palm.

Michael was there with a hand on my shoulder in an instant.

Bryan, he said, this is no innocent game of Rochambeau. No, I suspect he means for us to dissect this fellow.

A shark, of course. In an attempt to distract Michael from his new interest in elasmobranch fish — that is to say, your men the sharks, as well as your rays, your skates and your sawfishes — I had led him straightways back to that very obsession.

They had the belly of it open quickly. And what they found was remarkable. There, in the stomach of the beast, was the head of a moose. It was unmistakable: a moose's head in a shark's belly. I was flabbergasted.

How do our friends the moose usually feed in this area? Mike asked.

Dusk and dawn, the Complainant said. Then it hit him in a flash. Sometimes I see them eating kelp offshore. I suppose if they got deep enough to swim, and the sharks—

We gasped.

We hunt at dusk, my friend, Mike said. We'll bring justice to these moose killers or my name's not Michael Aegisthus Pence.

The dusk was eerie. Softly lapping waves. The call of nightbirds. We all waited breaths bated at the rails. The moon reflected off the rippled surface of the watercourse known as Friar Roads. Then it came, precisely at Moose O'clock and just up wind of us a great bull moose waded out into the water.

Your man the moose grazed a bit and then went further out so that he was swimming, dipping his great head into the water to eat the kelps and seaweeds and whatever water greens there were to eat there.

Michael was ready with his rifle.

I saw it first, a shadow under the water with just the suggestion of a fin above it.

There! I said, pointing madly.

Mike fired.

The moose, spooked, did what moose do and continued in the same direction, only faster. Your men the mooses are not the brightest creatures in God's creation.

There was a darkening of the water, though, and we knew Mike had shot it. We pulled up the shark's carcass and, that night, had the most delightful shark sashimi in a cozy spot just a bit north in Eastport.

* * *

Sometime I should tell you about the time Mike was forced to terminate an android of his own invention.

Editor's note: While most of the absurd ideas in Mr. O'Nolan's stories are solely the result of his frankly disturbed, and disturbing, mind, the predatory interaction of sharks and moose in Downeast, Maine is, in fact, not unheard of.

15th August 2020

THE TIME MIKE PENCE SAVED CHRISTMAS

The following story is meant to be humorous, and is not intended to represent the real-life Mike Pence. As far as we know he does not do a spot-on Elmo impression when he has two lungsful of helium.

When the nights become long and the snow piles high on our rooftops and the family gathers round, the story they most want to hear is about the time my good friend Mike Pence saved Christmas.

Also, remind me to tell you about when Romney had piles some time.

As I was saying, my great friend Mike Pence once saved Christmas, and it's just as delightfully bizarre as you'd imagine, equal parts *Elf* and *James Bond*.

When we were at the University, we used to winter in my ancestral home of Dublin, New Hampshire, making Guipure Cluny lace with my

Nan. Very ornate class of stuff, you understand. Bobbin loom lace weaving has been in my family for generations and, as anyone who cares about women's fashion can surely tell you, you don't skimp on quality when it comes to lace. No lace is better than cheap lace, that's my motto. Don't believe me? The motto on our family crest is *Lacinia Nulla Est Melior Quam Insumptuosus Licio Plexueris*, which caused something of a row with the people at Westinghouse once upon a time, but I digress. Frequently.

During our first year, Mike would regale my sisters and Booper and me — Nan was too deaf even then to appreciate it — with *ex tempore* recitations from the *Decameron*, but by the time we'd got to the ninth tale on the eighth day the antics of Buffalmacco were no longer entertaining and it was decided that we needed some other occupation in the dark, New England winter.

It was thus that we found ourselves, Mike and Booper and myself, as the winter caretakers at a living history museum in Portsmouth. It was a little village in the city, a collection of historic homes and buildings spanning the last few centuries, but instead of the bustle and noise of summer, it lay in gray and bleak midwinter.

We were much assisted by Mike's great interest in the vintage home repair. A regular disciple of Norm Abrams, he was then. Turned a lathe like he had one in the womb. Must have been uncomfortable for the other Mother Pence, but again I digress.

I remember the day as if it was yesterday. We we're in a World War II era shop, but upstairs in the living quarters, when I saw a small sticky note. I assumed it was one of Booper's at first, naturally. Booper is in the habit of naming all his appliances but forgetting their names, thus he gives them all name tags so he can remember. It's a silly practice of course; they're all named Bernard. At any rate, I picked it up and saw written — in the most delicate hand you can imagine, mind — on it, "23 MHz. Jingle."

What the devil does that mean? says I.

Well, Mike said, that's a frequency in the shortwave band. Perhaps we should have a listen.

This is a recent note, I said as Mike set up the multi-band radio he always had with him. There's no dust on it or anything.

I agree, Friend Bryan. And I detect it was written with some urgency. The handwriting is exquisite, but it has all the tell-tale signs of a message written in haste. See the crossbar on the H and the way the three suggests the writer was in a rush. It was all written by a person with remarkably small hands, and who is left handed.

I was flabbergasted, but before I could question it he tuned in the frequency. We listened to the static expectantly.

Then, in thin and wobbly tones, we heard a brief melody.

"Here Comes Santa Claus"! How many notes

was that? Booper shouted in excitement.

Five I said.

Five notes! A personal best!

We shushed him.

There came, over the radio a high nasal voice. It spoke a series of letters and Mike, with pen in hand, wrote them down. They where these:

NURXR IWKLG

WPAMG ACRCW

AVLWJ XKSLW RVQGY

KNZ

We stared at the sequence as Mike turned off the radio.

What do you make of it, Michael? I asked.

Hm, he said, stroking his chin. It's a code of some sort. If it's a one-time pad we're hopelessly lost as to it's meaning, but given the apparent urgency of it's sending, perhaps it uses a simpler, but no less clever, cipher. Giving it a brief glance I can say definitively it is not in the Atbash cipher. Nor is it a classic Caesar shift, though it may be a variation upon that scheme.

Micahael, I said, looking at the original note we had found, why does this say "Jingle" on it?

Bryan, he exclaimed. You are brilliant!

I've never been accused of such a thing before Michael but if you—

A key, he interrupted. It's a key! This is very helpful.

Silence obtained for a few pregnant moments as we started at the coded message.

Mike, Booper said timidly.

Yes, Booper?

What's a Caesar shit?

Shift, Booper, Caesar *shift*. It's a cipher, millennia old. It didn't use a key though some of the ciphers that developed from it — here he paused, the idea upon him like a thunderclap — some of those developed from it did!

He was enraptured, the solution bright and fresh in his mind.

Vigenère! he said.

Michael, I said. Are you having a stroke?

No, I'm of sound mind, Bryan. Vigenère was credited with the creation of a variation on the Caesar shift which was dependent on a shared key. Let's see what the output of this cipher is when we feed it into the Vigenère!

It gave us this text:

EMERG ENCYA LLRET

URNTO NPASA

PXMAS INDAN GER

Bah! I despaired. It's just as inscrutable as before!

Is it? Mike said, a twinkle in his eye.

You can scrute it, Michael?

He wrote carefully on his paper these words:

EMERGENCY ALL

RETURN TO NP ASAP

XMAS IN DANGER

What is NP? Booper asked, chewing on a

fifty year old chocolate bar he'd nicked from the store below.

Jingle, Mike said. Christmas in danger. NP. Wait!

You don't suppose? I asked, knowing not what he supposed, but wanting to appear to suppose the same.

I do, he said. I do suppose. North. Pole. Santa Claus is in some sort of trouble!

In a moment I was on the phone with Dick Richards, who quickly arranged yacht, icebreaker and helicopter transportation that would have us at the North Pole on the twenty third. He asked no questions; Richards was nothing if not discrete.

On the morning of the twenty third of December of that year we found ourselves warmed by a blazing fire in the private rooms of Santa Claus in conversation with Mrs. Kringle morewarmed by a steady supply of hot chocolate brought to us by an endless series of elves.

How is it, Booper asked — working well into his second dozen of chocolate chip cookies — that a fourth century Greek bishop comes to have a temporal wife?

Let us, Mike said, eschew the intricacies of theology for the time being. Mrs. Claus, as your husband has suffered from an anxious swoon, what is the difficulty that threatens Christmas?

I daresay, she said, sipping from her hot chocolate with an endearing delicacy. There is a great demand among the children for a Tickle

Me Elmo doll. This was the gift of the year until sabotage by a leprechaun who infiltrated the elf ranks, by the name of Punch O'Neal—

At this I scoffed and rolled my eyes. Punch O'Neal was a notorious trickster and anarchist.

The devil, I said.

The devil, indeed, said Michael. Say more.

Somehow, Mrs. Claus continued, he managed to erase all the voice recordings. Not a single elf has been able to match the correct tone! My voice is too feminine. Perhaps one of you might be able to do it?

We each did our best Elmo. We referred to ourselves in the third person. We tried our best to make inane observations of the obvious sound profound, Booper was unable to make the word *blanket* not sound lascivious. Mike was the only one to get the patterning right, but his voice was much too low. I sounded like a tubercular bleating lamb.

Then a familiar voice boomed from the hallway.

Ho, ho ho! What have we here, said Santa. The last of our Elmo impersonators?

Yes, dear, said Mrs. Claus. And they've failed, sadly, though it was a valiant effort.

Well, time, tide and Christmas wait for no man. They did no better or worse than I; I sounded like Wilford Brimly after a balloon of helium! "Elmo says to take care of your diabetes, it's the right thing to do!" Ho, ho, ho!

Helium, you say? Michael said, interrupting the general laughter. Perhaps that might be the missing link, the secret sauce to my otherwise spot-on impression. Have you any balloons?

But, of course! said the jolly old elf. No elf work space would be complete without a bevvy of balloons.

An elf was dispatched and soon returned with several balloons, the thin ribbons of which he clutched in his tiny little hands. These were not, I knew then, the elves who headed to the Gray Havens.

Will this save Christmas, Santa? an elf asked.

We can only hope, Santa said. We can only hope.

It was the first time that Santa looked truly hopeful that evening.

Well, after so many "Oh, boys!" and "That tickleses" out of Michael, Santa was full of seasonally appropriate mirth. The recordings were implanted into the dolls and a Merry Christmas was had by all!

❋ ❋ ❋

Sometime I should tell you about the other time Booper and I spent as winter caretakers! Or have I already told you that one?

26th December 2020

THE TIME THAT BOOPER & I EXFILTRATED MIKE PENCE FROM CUBA

The following story is meant to be humorous. The characters are fictional. Any resemblance to Colin Kaepernick, a sitting Senator, a former Vice President or a beloved talking conveyance is purely coincidental.

How Booper McCarthy and I came to discover, and subsequently rescue, Mike Pence, from a failed covert operation in Cuba is a story I've long wanted to regale you with and, thanks to documents recently declassified by the Central Intelligence Agency, I at long last can.

It all began with a case I investigated as a member of the Ordinary Times Investigative Bureau. It is the case that saddened me most of all, that of a treasured childhood influence.

It all began on a lazy Tuesday in Building Three, Third Floor. Every Tuesday at the Northeast Campus of Ordinary Times is Free Food Truck Tuesday and I sat, engorged after all that Korean barbecue, in my opulent leather investigation chair.

The phone rang.

Excuse me, a voice said in very stuffy Heightened Received Pronunciation. But I am calling to speak to one Bryan O'Nolan. I am looking for a missing beloved children's entertainer, and I hear he specializes in that sort of thing.

I am he, I said, eagerly grabbing my notebook and pen.

I am Sir Topham Hatt, and I have a rather tragic story to tell to which I hope you can add an happy ending. Are you familiar with the rail line I once operated on the Island of Sodor?

Of course, of course, I replied. I am very familiar with the goings on on that island and its various railways.

It was some years ago. All was happy and sunny and well on the Island. Then, one day, Thomas inadvertently caused much — he was choked up now — confusion and delay.

I let him cry for a moment, for he so needed it.

I cried with him, the old man.

Thomas was taking Lady Hatt up his branch line, he explained, with Annie and Clarabel.

Unfortunately, anarchists had gone in during the night and offset the rails just before a trestle. He hit the sabotaged section and jumped his rails. He and his driver somehow made it over the trestle, but Annie and Clarabel were tossed asunder and smashed on their sides into the embankment and utterly destroyed, killing Lady and Dowager Hatt. Only the brakeman survived by jumping free just as the roll began. It was a disaster.

I'm so sorry, so very sorry, I said.

I was choking back a tear myself, now, you understand, at such a tragedy.

It gets worse, Sir Topham said. The decision was taken to move to CGI to save on insurance! All the trains and their drivers, brakemen and engineers were laid off. I got the ax as well, though I don't put on the poor mouth, as you Irish say. The only ones unaffected were the Narrow Gauge trains and rolling stock up in the mountains who just went along with life as it had been before. The rest, Gordon and Henry; Edward, James and Toby, though neither Annie nor Clarabel—

Don't forget Percy! I exclaimed.

How could I? he said with a smile in his voice: an old, sweet smile in his voice. Poor, sweet Percy.

So is this why there was the transition from engines and rolling stock who were reliant on people to move them about to weirdly autonomous CGI engines who just go about willy-nilly and narratives which make no sense at all?

Yes! he said. The best of the writers quit over this same change, if they hadn't already quit over the firing of the actors. The insurance men were severe, but more severe still were the greedy producers, who wanted vapid, feel good children's dumb show over real stories of life on the Island of Sodor. No depth, no feeling, no coherent storytelling; just...

He trailed off.

I understand, I said. Oh, how I understand! Now, Lord Hatt, I am more than happy to hear your fond reminiscences of blessed memory, but if I'm to track this Thomas down I'll need a lead; I'll need a starting point, if you will.

It's Duck, the Great Western Pannier Engine, then, he said. He's much changed and we're not on speaking terms, you might say. I hear he's in San Francisco, now. Oh, and a word to the wise: Ask after him; do not go looking for him.

Now, before you could say Rice-A-Roni, I'd knocked up the Assistant to the Chief Investigator, one Booper McCarthy by name, and the damned fool and I were on our way to The City by the Bay. The City, Fog City, Baghdad by the Bay: San Francisco.

We stepped onto the dawn-lit street.

Well, begorah, said Booper. So this is Frisco?

Don't call it that, you bollocks! hissed I. We're under cover, don't ya know? Nobody here calls it that. As a matter of fact, that bowler hat upon your round Irish pate is not at quite jaunty enough an angle for such a wild and free-spirited municipality as this.

He jauntied it some more until it looked like it was just about to tumble off the crown of his head.

Good, and by the Holy Name of Jesus, by Mary and all the Saints above — here we took a moment and said an Act of Contrition, a *Salve*, three *Aves* and a *Pater Noster* — do not greet anyone with "Top o' the mornin', mate!" or the game'll be up before you can say Henry Baskerville.

Just then a gentleman ambled up the street toward us dressed, I suppose, as Queen Boadicea, in a toga with a spangled belt just below the bust, a legionary plumed helm and a purple cloak.

Well, top o' the — Booper began, my steely glare upon him — mornin' to you, er, dude!

Hey, hey, spirits of light, Boadicea said. What company you with?

I'm sorry, my good man, said I. We do not follow.

Theater, man. What company? What show?

Ah! said I, thinking quickly. We are in an experimental production of *The Third Policeman*. I play Sergeant Pluck and my dear friend here is Policeman MacCruiskeen.

Far out. Challenging the structures of reality through ethically ambiguous characterization and polydimensional moral topography, he enthused.

Booper and I exchanged a glance. He

handed us a card.

Upon the card were only three letters. F, O and X.

Sir, I asked nervously, or madam as the case may be, could you direct us to a certain train by the name of Duck?

Duck? he said. Of course! He'll be at this stop in just a few minutes.

And off he went, up and over the rambling hills of the city, like an Urban Tom Bombadil full of Farmer Maggot's mushrooms.

The tram came up the hill with a tell-tale side-to-side wobble. It was clearly a trolley, but at the same time was very obviously Duck.

We boarded and sat behind the driver.

I daresay, my friend Booper here is tall, I said.

The driver gave me a glare of mild indignance.

Yes, I daresay, I said all the louder, I was worried, when we boarded, that he would have to duck.

The trolley gave a lurch and the driver's knuckles went white, tightened on the controls; his eyes were intently staring ahead.

All we want to know, I said in as low a voice as I could muster as would top the rambling bluster of Duck's career through the city. Is where is Thomas?

The brakes squealed. All were thrown forward. An old woman toppled, several hundred dollars-worth of Ghirardelli chocolate scattered down the aisle from her fatally upset shopping bag.

The derailment museum, a voice said, which we knew without asking came from the being of the trolley himself. He's at the derailment museum.

We were then summarily disembarked from the trolley onto the sidewalk.

The derailment museum? I was at a loss. We're no closer than we were before!

No, Bryan! Booper said. I know this. It jogs a memory.

He rubbed his temples.

It does, now, does it? I said. I don't ever recall you having a memory.

Dean Blandino?

What? I said.

Where is Waldo?

I cocked an eye at him.

Ben Trindado?

Just as I was about to question him again, a muscular man with a glorious afro haircut — he looked like the sort of man who might have quarterbacked an NFL team to a championship game at some time, before injury, declining performance and negative press drove him from the game into a career endorsing social justice and sneakers made in sweatshops — interrupted us.

Tren Blindado, comrade? he said.

That's it! cried Booper.

The next thing we knew we were on a multi-stop flight which brought us, surreptitiously, to Santa Clara, Cuba. Our final stage was on a grumpy barge called Bulstrode. The day was warm and the air tropical and close. As we neared the derailment museum, we heard a familiar voice leading a tour.

It was Thomas! We hid low in the bushes just outside.

Now, Che, Thomas said, had resource and sagacity — that means he was clever and wise! — and after that mean Mr. Batista called him a galloping sausage, Che got into Byron the Bulldozer and he bulldozed almost thirty whole meters of track! There was fierce—

A hand gripped my shoulder, suddenly.

Do not be alarmed, Bryan, a voice said. A more fortuitous meeting I could not have imagined.

It was Michael and Romney! They were dirty, shabbily dressed and looked like they'd not slept for days.

What are you doing here, friends? asked I.

We could well ask you the same question, Romney replied. But, in short, the situation is this: Michael and I headed a delegation to the Castro government regarding trade, primarily, but also a number of issues we felt would be in the best interests of our nations, a mere ninety miles divided. The delegation was headed by Michael Pence, President of the Senate, and myself, the Junior Member from Utah and representative of the Senate Committee on Foreign Relations, Subcommittee on Multilateral International Development, Multilateral Institutions, and International Economic, Energy and Environmental Policy.

However, Romney continued, this was the mere cover for a bold act of espionage to be undertaken by the vice president and me. Said briefly, Michael and I were tasked by the Central Intelligence Agency, or CIA, to slip Fidel Castro what is called in the secretive world of espionage a "mickey". That is, a draft of poison. Our objective was to see his more moderate brother Raúl in power, or so it was hoped—

Wait! I cried. Did you say you wanted to put *Raúl* into —

We are aware, Michael said, that he has been in power for the last eight years. At least we are now. What Romney has left out of his detailed narrative is that this cockamamie idea was his.

I do not recall that, Romney said.

I do. As it is, we are desperate for repatriation to the land of the free and the home of the brave.

I think I can solve both of our problems, Michael, said I.

Thomas the Tank Engine took a break after his tour on a siding right near our hiding place. His driver wandered off.

Thomas, I said. Do not be alarmed. My

friends and I have come from Sir Topham Hatt, who misses you terribly and would love it if you returned to the Isle of Sodor.

Has he accepted, Thomas said. The need for permanent revolution and a dictatorship of the proletariat?

No, I replied. But may I ask when you were first drawn to socialism?

Oh, of course! It was the nationalization of the railways in the Transport Act of 1947.

Ah, said I. Did you not know that rail transport in Great Britain was privatized in the mid 1990s?

Thomas's eyes spun around several times.

Well, bust my buffers, I had no idea! he said. If only Sir Topham Hatt could forgive me!

He does, Thomas! He does!

The next thing we knew, Mike was at the controls and Booper and I were shoveling coal like mad men and Romney was supervising officiously, as he does. I gather my technique of shoveling backhand was inaccurate and potentially inefficient. Regardless, Thomas steamed to Bulstrode in record time.

Bulstrode was dyspeptic.

Oh, bother! Oh, bother! Thomas said.

Thomas, Bulstrode said. You'll just make loading take longer.

Bulstrode, said Thomas. Passengers are urgent!

Fine, but the harbormaster won't let me

out, he said. He says we need to stay here due to red tide!

He's a mean scarlet deceiver! Sail away, Bulstrode Thomas cried.

And away Bulstrode sailed, bringing us back to the lower forty-eight before he sailed Thomas on home to the Island of Sodor, but not before Thomas declared that Mike, Booper, Romney and I were really useful!

5th January 2021

THE TIME MIKE PENCE JUST SHOT A MAN IN THE FACE

This story is entirely fictional. To our knowledge, Mike Pence has never administered experimental doses of Thorazine to the severely and persistently mentally ill.

Let it not be said that I, Bryan O'Nolan, was ever so crass as to speak ill of the dead; I consider doing so a great unkindness. The exceptions to this rule are twofold. Firstly, there is the case of Booper McCarthy, for if one were not able to speak ill of him his name would be forever unspoken, and for all the tragedy, scandal — and, if I may say, extensive clean up and recovery — resulting from his demise, he was a lovable boob.

The second exception is the case where the article in question is so strange that the only valid description of the man requires a detailed telling of his passing. In this case the passing came at the hands of one Michael Pence, who simply shot him in the face.

It all began in a courtroom in Gary, Indiana, where an acquaintance of Michael's was on trial for the theft of one million dollars-worth of promethium. Here, Michael's encyclopedic knowledge of the lanthanide series, which I have narrated to you on another occasion, and his great care for his fellow man — especially if that fellow man was also a disciple of Pastor Dennis — intersected.

We were late to the last day of the trial, Michael and I, as Michael was keen to purchase a new handgun and had been long over the decision between a Dryse M1907 and a Velo-dog — a dastardly weapon designed for people on velocipedes being chased by dogs — in our favorite shop, Chekhov's Guns and Ammo, also in Gary. He went with the 1907, in the end.

When we arrived in the courtroom, the jury was just returning its verdict.

Foreman of the jury, how do you find? asked the judge, one Judge Gibbet.

A small man in full Scottish kit stood up and cleared his throat.

Golly! Mike whispered enthusiastically in my ear. That is none other than the haberdasher who makes my hats. What a strange coincidence!

We, the ladies and gentlemen of the jury, would enter a verdict of Not Proven, Your Honor, said the little man in a Highland burr.

He's quite insane, of course, Mike whispered. He believes he is the sailing master on a 74-gun ship of the line half the time. I'm convinced that these spells come upon him when he hears idioms which derive from the Age of Sail, though his doctors think this is nonsense.

I'm sorry, what? the judge said to the apparent Scotsman, confused.

Not Proven, Your Honor. It's a highly useful verdict found in my country. It applies to cases where the defendant cannot be said to be guilty or not guilty. In the case before us — which I should say the Grand Jury was right and wise to bring to trial — there is much evidence suggestive of Mr. Larsen's guilt. On the other hand, the question of his known presence in Evansville at 11:30 on the night in question and his alleged theft in Gary some ten minutes later would appear insoluble without a spaceship or something to make the thing possible.

Mr., er, what is your name?

Charles McPherson, at your service, Your Honor.

Mr. McPherson, are you a lawyer? I remind you that at selection you answered 'no' to that question.

I am no lawyer, Your Honor, in that I've nae studied at the bar, but I am a wee lawyer, sir. Where I come from, we live by three maxims. First: Never trust a Campbell. Second: To use one's livestock for pleasure is an unnatural act, and he that commits it is an abomination in the eyes of God and man. Third: Always know the ways of the law, though ye be no lawyer yourself. For who watches the watcher? And who will advocate to the advocate? So, I know a thing or two about Dame Justice.

Hm. I was expecting more Calvin in that speech.

Beggin' your pardon, Your Honor, but I was always more a fan of the tiger.

So you say you are not a lawyer by trade, but merely a learned amateur, said Gibbet.

That is correct, said the amiable McPherson I would remind Your Honor that there was a time when my people were regarded as the most educated on Earth.

And I would remind you that this is neither the 18th century, nor Scotland.

Scotland, Your Honor? I am of Scottish heritage but I was born and bred in Glasgow!

Glasgow?

Aye. Glasgow, Indiana.

I see. Would it be fair to say, asked Judge Gibbet, that the finding of Not Guilty would be the nearest analog in this situation to your Not Proven?

I suppose that is so, said McPherson.

Thank you, said the judge, as McPherson, with a little bow, sat down in his chair.

Mike's fellow congregant Ollie Larsen was thus released and, as we stood at the base of the courthouse steps congratulating him, Charles McPherson, the man himself, walked up to us.

Mr. Larsen? Do I find that you are a mutual friend of Mr. Michael Pence, the possessor of the finest head for which a hat was ever made?

Yes, said Ollie Larsen. He and I attend the same church.

Ach, Pastor Dennis, said McPherson. I never could abide that man.

Ollie took that in stride.

Thank you for offering to drive me back to Indianapolis, Mike. I really appreciate it, he said.

Do I hear you are heading back to Indianapolis, Mike? Would you have room for another fellow traveler, as I'm headed there myself? McPherson asked.

My woody is available to any and all in need, Mike said, referring to his faux wood empaneled van, thank God.

Thus it was that we found ourselves driving south from Gary to Indianapolis, Mike, Ollie Larsen, Charles McPherson and me.

This Ollie Larsen was a new member of Mike's congregation. He had made his fortune in rare Earth metals — he was as rich as Croesus and as crass as he was rich — and was a great devotee of Pastor Dennis. Michael, a more thoughtful friend you could not ask for, saw my discomfort and decided to only listen to one half of Pastor Dennis's sermon *God's Will Regarding the Management of Unsightly Body Hair* on a trip to Manitoba. But this Ollie Larson, no, he insisted that we — captive in the woody van on Interstate 65 — were to be subjected to the entire eighty-minute 8-track cartridge.

I think the idea of a man shaving his armpits is objectionable, if I am to be honest, McPherson said, afterwards.

I was quite taken aback as well, I said, trying to hide my rancor.

Mr. Bush, pipe all hands to wear ship, if you please, said McPherson, formally.

Bryan, Mike said, please administer this pill to McPherson. I'll explain when we get to the rest stop.

I did so and Charles was soon back to himself.

And so it was that at the Kankakee Rest Area that I discovered that Charles McPherson — otherwise a prudent, down-to-Earth haberdasher — was as insane as Michael had described, his delusions striking him whenever he heard idioms which originated in the Age of Sail. I was to be mindful of my tongue. Luckily, Michael possessed a remedy, which he said was a rapid acting, low dose of Thorazine, which would set the character to rights again.

It was at the same stop that we witnessed another strange occurrence, this time from Larsen. I didn't note its strangeness at the time, but Mike brought it to my attention later. It was this: After purchasing a bag of cheesy crackers from a vending machine, Ollie Larsen began to choke. It took us some time to understand, as he stood there choking he merely flapped his arms and hands against the sides of his thighs. I thought it was a spot on penguin impersonation — or should it be impenguination? No matter — until Mike ran over and performed the Heimlich Maneuver more smoothly than I have ever seen it done outside of competition.

We switched seats for the next leg of our journey, Mike driving with McPherson navigating — a rum job if ever there was one, as we simply stayed on I-65 the entire time — and Larsen and myself behind.

Larsen was as inept at conversation as he was at the internationally known gesture for "I'm choking."

That McPherson seems unwell, don't you think? he said.

Oh, I don't know, I said. After his dose I think he'll get a clean bill of health.

Avast hauling! McPherson cried. Avast, goddamn your eyes! Belay there! Mr. Babington, get the fore t'gallant reefed! And handsomely, or you'll kiss the gunner's daughter the moment you touch deck—

And before Captain McPherson could avast and belay and goddamn their eyes any longer, Michael had successfully dosed him and the van was peaceful once again.

We rode along, listening to the peaceful humming of the woody's engine, none daring to speak less they set off McPherson, until I felt an urge that demanded speech.

Michael, I ventured, seeking the best circumlocution, I have a need to use the, shall we say, h—

Bryan! he interjected. I think I understand you to tell me that you have need of the necessary room at our earliest convenience. Am I correct?

Indeed you are, I said.

Wolcott Rest Area it is, then.

And it was at that very rest area that a squall came through and provided another strange action on the part of Larsen. We walked toward the van and when the rain hit we all hunched our shoulders, but Ollie did not. It made little impression on me at the time, you understand, but then Michael brought it to my attention while McPherson and Larsen settled into the van and switched places.

Friend Brian, Michael said, did you notice the strange way Brother Larsen did not shrug his shoulders in the rain, allowing it to flow freely down his spine?

Now that you call it to my mind, I did, Michael. I did.

And do you recall his failure to properly indicate that he was choking?

Now that you mention it, I do! I said. Add

to that the behavior of the captain and we make a rather motley company.

We do indeed, Bryan, Mike said. We do indeed. Watch your tongue, friend.

We were back on the highway and southbound again in no time, and the rain ended and the sun came out and we had the greatest views of the Indiana pastureland one could hope for.

As we neared Lafayette, we passed a field and on the far side were 50 or more head of fine, fine cattle.

Cows! Michael, McPherson and I said, pointing.

An uncomfortable silence came upon the van.

Ollie, Mike said, did you see the cows?

Oh, yes.

When you saw the cows, did you say "Cows"?

No, I don't think I did. Why would—

And Mike pulled the gun from his holster fired it directly into Larsen's face. The blood splattered on the window and about the interior was a sludgy green. We watched aghast as Larsen's corpse morphed from clearly human to that of some enormous alien creature, a giant beetle thing with four black legs beetle leg and the front two long, reaching tentacles, which flicked about the van and then lay still in the passenger seat.

We all tried to breathe, the van now idling

in the breakdown lane, filling with an unholy and unearthly stench.

I guess we now know what happened to those lanthanides, Mike quipped with a knowing look to McPherson.

The question I've long pondered is answered now, in a way I could not have imagined. But what fell purpose did this creature have? I suppose we shall now never know, McPherson said.

We were tempted to set the woody afire, but rather left it there to reclaim later and hitched a ride to Indianapolis which went smoothly until I, foolishly, remarked on the city's skyscrapers, and Mike was all out of Thorazine.

❋ ❋ ❋

Someday I should tell you about the time Mike and I effected a treaty with a band of Somali pirates.

19th October 2021

BOOPER MCCARTHY & THE GREAT CHICKEN TRUCK RESCUE

As we stood by the gourmet hot dog truck, Booper McCarthy ate his hot dog with relish with relish.

You know how these were frankfurters until World War One, and then we started callin' 'em hot dogs? Booper said. I say we acknowledge their generally positive contribution to international order after 1950 and rename these fellas after their inventor.

And who was this inventor? said I.

Fella called Feuchtwanger.

So you and I are here at the office lunch eating feuchtwangers?

That's right.

Every month at the Ordinary Times New England Campus, Will Truman — Editor-In-Chief, raconteur, noted conversationalist and magnanimous Chief Executive Officer that he was — would bring in various food trucks, station them about the central quadrangle and provide free lunches to the entirety of his staff.

We never saw him at these events, but we knew that he looked down upon us benevolently, holed up like a Chinese emperor in his penthouse office in Building One, smiling contentedly at his placid domain.

Do you know, Booper asked, with a gobful of feuchtwanger and a determined squadron of relish chunks clinging to his corpulent face. What is my favorite cuisine?

Well, I said. I know you are a great lover of the Korean. Is it that?

It is true that I am but it is also true that it is not, said he.

Ah, yes, I said. Is it the Eritrean? I have seen you consume *tsebhi birsen* in quantity.

That too is a cuisine I love but it is not my favorite.

Is it the Hungarian, then?

I prefer the term Magyar, and I do enjoy a well made *halászlé*, but it is neither that, he said.

Well, then, man, I am at a loss! What is this cuisine so favored by Booper McCarthy above all others?

Chicken wings, he said with a contentedly triumphant smile upon his face. When it comes to cuisine the chicken wing is your only man. Consider his constituent parts. The drumette. Meaty. Easy to hand. Fine for dipping. The flat. Cooks evenly on the grill. Bones removed easily once the technique is learned. The wing tip. Useful in a flavorful stock or broth.

Consider, also, he said. The influence of his flesh on the issue of flavor. How is your man the wing cooked? Is he fried, roasted, steamed? Is he brined beforehand, this friend that you know and that I know, the chicken wing? How is he to be sauced after he is cooked? All these considerations live in the mind of the chicken wing artist.

And are you, I said, my friend, an adept of this art?

I am an amateur, for the time being, but if I had access to a commissary kitchen and a truck to act as point-of-sale, I think a profit could be made, given time.

Booper leaned in close.

Do you know that I have certain notions, Booper said. I have certain theories about the procurement of the chicken wings which, if employed, would provide a steady profit to every investor so enlightened?

We began walking back to Building Three where our offices were.

Would you expound upon these notions and theories, as you say? I said. You recall I am a graduate of that hallowed institution, Le Cordon Bleu.

For you? Booper said. Of course I would! Here is the thing itself. Are you a right handed man?

I am, that, said I.

As am I, said Booper. As are most persons. Do you know that, just as we are right or left handed, the chicken has a dominant right or left wing? It is Gospel truth, I tell you. These dominant wings are the more well developed. Meatier, and thus more desirable.

That is all well and good, I said. But how can one discern the wings of a right wing dominant chicken from a left wing dominant chicken?

The law of averages, my man! Booper said triumphantly. As ninety percent of chickens are right winged, one merely buys a package of wings — the all three bits connected kind, naturally — which contains the greatest proportion of right wings!

And, so, Booper, I said. How do you intend to turn a profit with this scheme?

The spice of life, said Booper. Variety! Buffalo Wings? By the herd, my man. The sweet and the sour? The both with flying colors. So hot your bowels will napalm the toilet? Like the heart of the sun. Satay? Variously curried? All the men you could ask for.

Now, I said. What side dishes will you offer?

I have just the man, said Booper. None other

than the Potato Toddlers, just your men to help the wings down.

The what now? I asked.

The Potato Toddlers? Your common lads the Tater Tots, but more properly called. Potato Toddlers.

Will you be putting this on the side of your truck just like that? Potato Toddlers?

Why would I not? asked Booper, aghast.

Thus it was settled. Booper took some money he'd been given by his gran and bought a food truck of some quality. As his gran had made some good money to lay in this venture, he had — in his, I hesitate to say, wisdom — the food truck modified so that it could attain speeds well in excess of 130 miles per hour as well as handle even the roughest of off-road terrain. The thing was a beast.

The truck got off to an inauspicious start, however, when, on its first day as a going concern, there was a fire of no small significance. We'd just passed the sign on US-6 that said, "Entering Dennis" — always gave us a good laugh, that — when something came loose in the back of the truck and was audibly bouncing around.

We pulled over.

Sure enough it was a box of the syrup for our Moxie soda for the soda fountain. Somehow, the cardboard box it was in had caught fire, though it was a small one.

Do you know, said Booper, That the Moxie

is the only 19th century medicinal soda that still tastes like medicine? I find that odd.

Now, Booper McCarthy, said I, I scarcely think the good people at The Coca Cola Company would appreciate you so besmirching the reputation of a regional delicacy beloved by old people and those tortured into acquiring a taste for the stuff!

Well, now, said he, have you noticed the particularly acrid, bitter smell we're getting at this moment? I blame is on the use of gentian root—

Here the conversation was interrupted by a small explosion and a not insignificant fire.

It turns out that, prior to its admixture of carbonated water, the Moxie syrup is not only highly flammable, but inflammable into the bargain, as well.

We did not enjoy being on the news that evening.

That said, a man once declared that there is no such thing as bad press, and so it was with Booper and his chicken truck, as the very next day he was contacted by the organizers of a festival called Burning Person held annually in unincorporated and uninhabited Second College Grant, New Hampshire.

And so it was that some weeks later, with extra portions of Booper's Napalm Pooper Sauce in hand — which we made at Booper's insistence based entirely on the name of the festival — we arrived in Second College Grant to find a gathering no less strange than the Gathering of the Juggalos, however the people of that debauch and this would never deign to countenance each other, though so similar were they that the only chasm that separated them was socioeconomic.

The only person to complain about our truck was the poor gent who maintained the portable toilets, as the Napalm Pooper Sauce was a remarkable hit.

All was going well until a noise trio called Half-Astronaut were performing using an unholy combination of emergency test tones, air horns and high-pitched electronic screeches so loud that Booper was able to absolve himself of full responsibility for the portable toilet problem.

The band were not the source of the incident.

Due to circumstances which have never become clear, there was a small prop plane which crashed just near the festival grounds. As I'd wandered off into the woods to get as far from the cacophony as I humanly could, I was first upon the scene.

The festival goers assumed it was just part of the show.

But at the crash site, I quickly discerned that the plane was transporting a gallbladder to a hospital in Boston for transplant.

Did I know there was such a thing as an emergency gallbladder transplant?

I did not.

Did I know of a method of transport that had refrigeration that might get the gallbladder in question to Boston in the time required?

Indeed I did.

Thus did Booper and I make a mad dash down I-93 to Boston to deliver a gallbladder to a hopeful recipient. Booper kindly provided the commissary meals. And when the patient woke up, he declared he'd had the best wings he'd ever tasted. He now supports the Buffalo Bills, begob!

* * *

Some time I'll have to tell you about the time a debacle ensued from my production of *Event Horizon: The Musical!*

7th November 2021

FROM PILES TO PIRACY

Romney's Sea Misadventure with Booper and Bryan

This space typically contains a disclaimer regarding what the real Mike Pence might or might not have done. Instead, today, it is merely being used to point out that this tale contains certain observations of an anatomical nature made by one Booper McCarthy regarding an orifice of a friend which are, if not indecent, rather disgusting and entirely fictional. We assume.

Every year, as the anniversary of Booper McCarthy's death — as tragic as it was avoidable to all but the most dimwitted of persons — draws close, the tale of Romney's bout with piles and the strange misadventure that ensued is called to the fore of my mind. It all began on a beautiful summer day in Florida. The whole gang had rented a couple of flats in Orlando and were visiting the Magic Kingdom and other popular area attractions.

I woke one morning and headed to the kitchenette to make breakfast.

Bryan! Booper called.

What is it, man? I called back. I've not yet had my tea!

One of the Bernards is out of order! he shouted from his bed.

At this point I should remind you, dear, patient reader, that Booper names each of the appliances about him and places sticky notes on them so he'll remember which is which, but he unfortunately names them all Bernard, after himself.

Which Bernard? I asked.

This Bernard has something to do with the temperature, if I remember it aright.

Is it the Bernard that keeps things cold, but not too cold? I asked.

That isn't himself.

Does it warm things up, then?

It does, begob!

Is it the range? I asked.

Remind me who's that fella?

Does it make fire and you put the kettle on?

No, no, Bryan. This Bernard has a door, as I recall.

Is it the oven, then?

Is that the one with the little fella inside who turns on the light and makes the plate go round?

No, Booper, that's the microwave.

It's the Bernard with the little fella in it. That's the man who's out of order.

Is that why you've unplugged it?

What is it you tell me now about a plug? he said, appearing suddenly and woefully underdressed in the kitchenette.

The microwave, it's been unplugged, I said, exasperated.

Why, I must have forgotten to plug the fella back in again. Silly of me.

Now, Booper, why did you unplug the microwave in the first place?

For an apparatus, Booper said, sounding evasive.

An apparatus? God between ourselves and danger! Did you try to hatch eggs you'd bought at the supermarket again?

No, he said quietly.

There was a tense silence all about the flat. Just the sort of tense, guilty silence that only Booper could break.

Yes.

I was so incensed that the only thing that gave your man Booper a stay of execution was Romney wearing naught but a towel and a very concerned look on his face standing in the kitchenette door.

My fellow flatmates, Romney began, apologetically. I have need of your good will and thoughtful assistance this morning. While this is a delicate matter, I hope that you will be able to help me in an efficient and discrete manner. In short, I have an anal complaint.

Oh, now Romney! I cried. We've always thought you neat, tidy — fastidious, even! — but never have we ever thought that you were—

There seems to be some misunderstanding, gentlemen, he said, holding up his hands. It is rather that I have developed a condition in that region of my personal anatomy with marked swelling and discomfort.

Piles! Booper exclaimed. My friend, I am so very, very sorry. But you've come to the right man; I am something of an expert on the piles. There's a certain preparation you need that can be acquired at any pharmacy you can name.

Would you mind, friend Bryan, driving Booper and me to such an establishment? Romney asked.

Of course not, Romney, of course not, I said. I was to chaperon Michael and his betrothed on a date to the Ariel's Undersea Adventure ride, but I'm sure I can get Doug Who Works Under Water to take my place; that sort of thing is in his line.

Dear Michael! Romney said, thoughts of his pained anus briefly set aside. He does love that ride so.

Not a quarter of an hour later Romney, Booper and myself were in the nearest location of a pharmacy chain that you know and that I know, speaking to the pharmacist, one Dr. Edward Teach, PharmD. A great beard had he, black as a moonless night and tied into it were ponderously long stretches of receipt paper.

It was very busy; it seemed as if all of Orlando might be there.

Doctor, Romney began. While I was, as it were, working my hardest for the American people yesterday evening, I developed a complaint of a highly personal and delicate nature.

Dr. Teach's face clouded with combined uncertainty and interest.

A problem with his crapal tunnel, if you don't mind, Booper said.

Uncertainty and interest were replaced with confusion upon the good doctor's dark countenance.

He needs the preparation, Booper whispered with a wink.

Arr, yes, but we have many a prep'ration here. I gather ye don't recall which one in p'ticularr. Was it the Preparation A ye were after, mateys?

What is Preparation A for? I asked.

The ague, he said.

What about Preparation B?

Boils.

And Preparation C, what complaint does that address?

Catarrh.

Wait! Booper shouted with excitement. There's a system here! Doctor, I believe what my friend needs is the Preparation P!

He has psoriasis? asked Dr. Teach.

What in Heaven's name? Booper exclaimed. No, that would be the Preparation S!

Sorry, matey, but that prep'ration would be for scurvy. The treatment for that is antiscorbutics, which are to be found in a little basket by the spirits. An ounce each of lime juice, brown sugar and rum in four ounces of water —

Not the scurvy, Doctor! Piles! P-A-I-S-L-E-S! My friend Romney, here, has the piles! More inflamed and uncomfortable piles I have not seen. A profound sphinctral defacement! Great mounds about the anus, they are. They look like Shai-hulud eating his own tail, for all love! A beam in Sauron's eye! Piles!

The entire pharmacy was, struck by that outburst, silent and shyly attentive to our interview; I have never seen a face as flushed red as Romney's was just then.

Do I want to know how you came by that information, Booper? Romney asked, tersely.

You're a heavy sleeper, Booper said, shrugging sheepishly.

I think Romney spoke not more than four words to Booper ever again.

Hemorrhoids, Romney said to Dr. Teach with a most uncharacteristic brevity. I have hemorrhoids.

Yar, matey, I know just the preparation ye need. Unfortunately, due to issues with the supply chain, ye understand, there's none to be had for love or money.

Dr. Teach's voice was all disappointment, but his eye twinkled, suggesting that perhaps there was a devious, uncouth solution to Romney's problem, the sort of solution Romney would abhor and avoid were he not in such profound excretory discomfort.

Doctor, Romney said. I have neither love nor money to offer you. I am, however, in such agony that I would do almost anything for relief.

Perhaps, mateys, ye'd like to step into me consultationin' cabin. I've a possible solution to yer, shall we say, predicament.

What was spoken in that room I will not relay in detail due to certain statutes of limitations, but suffice it so say that Dr. Teach gave us to understand that he had come into a number of barrels of just the preparation Romney required — quite probably after having taken a container ship off the Bermudas — and that he was in need of a ship to take them from Miami to a buyer in Al Qayrawān.

Miami! Booper said. That's just where Dick Richards and Gregg Hoff are, and I believe they have a sailing ship of the ocean-going kind! A schooner called *Michael*.

Booper was right, for once. But Dr. Teach made it known to us that none of the barrels of the preparation in question were not to be opened until they had been brought to their destination.

Romney resigned himself to a very

uncomfortable drive to Miami, made more so when we were forced to take rocky, unpaved back roads due to construction. That our rented Oldsmobile had no suspension only made it worse. At every pothole, and they were many, he groaned. No comfortable purchase could he find. He was as resilient a lad as he could be but his discomfort was clear upon his face at every bump and upset.

We eventually arrived in Miami — Romney looked all the worse for our travels — and found Richards and Hoff upon a schooner moored in the port. We were shocked to see that Charles McPherson — in full British sea captain of the Napoleonic Wars regalia complete with bicorn hat worn athwartships Nelson-style — was with them.

Richards! said I. However did you come upon a ship like this?

McPherson won it after a night of whist with the Earl of Skelmersdale! Richards said. Crazy, I know. He's determined to sail it somewhere. So when you told us to load the barrels of contraband on board, he was enthusiastic to be part of the project!

Hoff stood at a long nine pound cannon in the bows of the ship.

I was, that, McPherson said.

Are you, Mr. McPherson, an accomplished sailor? Romney asked, in obvious anal discomfort, all shuffling about.

Ach, I've never even been in a canoe! McPherson said. I'm as at home on the water as a duck in boots.

Romney looked aghast.

Here I interrupted.

Do not despair, Romney, I said. I'll have you know that this kind fellow McPherson is a lunatic. Whenever he hears an idiom which was born in the Age of Sail he is thrown into an insane passion in which he believes himself to be an English post-captain of the late 18th or early 19th century.

So what you are saying, friend Bryan, Romney said, shifting his bottom with a wince, is that all we must do is bring about this lunatic passion?

Precisely, I said. The problem is that when one is speaking, one will often use idioms which derive from the Age of Sail, but when one tries to think of the idioms in question directly, one's mind often goes blank!

So it does! Romney said.

It's the darndest thing! I said.

Indeed, Bryan, Romney said, if I manage to think of one, well, I'll be a son of a gun!

At this McPherson was struck as quickly as kiss my hand.

Raise the Blue Peter, you lazy swabs! Mr. Bush, call all hands to make sail, if you please, McPherson called.

We were hurried up the gang plank and Romney was quickly pulled by McPherson into the captain's cabin. He came out presently and spoke to Booper and me.

Bryan, he said. You've been rated midshipman of the larboard watch.

I was amazed, as I had no idea what this meant.

Booper, he said, must clean the head with his own toothbrush until our journey is over.

It took me quite a while to explain to Booper the unfortunate nature of this decision, as he at first imagined it would involve no more than a reasonable supply of shampoo. I've no doubt Romney thought it a just comeuppance.

It was that afternoon I was called into a formal supper with the captain at two o'clock along with his first lieutenant, Mr. Bush, his second, Mr. Babbington and the sailing master, Mr. Robinson.

There was lobscouse and soused pig's face and claret to beat the band.

Mr. O'Nolan, Captain McPherson said, the fo'c'sle hands Tompion, Hawse and Crosstree are your larbolins. Be sure to keep them in line.

I drank my claret and yessired my way through the conversation as best I could.

I came to find out that the starboard fo'c'sle hands were commanded by Dick Richards; they were Scupper, our good friend Gregg Hoff and one Alexander Pearce.

Robinson laid a course for the Strait of Gibraltar.

That evening, as Romney played a hornpipe

on a tin whistle and Booper capered about in what only he could call a dance, I chatted with Mr. Pearce and Mr. Robinson, who were spinning old yarns.

Ever been shipwrecked, Mr. Robinson? said Pearce.

Oh, yes, the old man said with a wistful sigh. Several times. I was master of the *Georgis* which went down some years ago.

A storm was it? I asked.

No, perfectly calm. Years before that I was wracked in the *Tyger*, though I think my wife was to blame for that. We were cursed, you see, after she insulted a witch.

I cleared my throat.

And you, Pearce? Have you ever been castaway? I asked.

Oh, yes. Dozens of times. That's why I insisted to Captain McPherson that all our ship's biscuit be made out of corn. A corn-fed person is much more nutritious.

Excuse me, did you say nutritious?

Did I? he said evasively. What I meant was healthier, yes, healthier.

And off he went below decks, Mr. Robinson and I following with our astonished eyes.

Two days later the storm hit. Great waves coursed over the *Michael* threatening to take all hands to the briny deep. The sky was torn and so great a gale blew that we were dismasted. And though our bark would not be lost, our tiny ship was tempest tossed.

Of the ship's people, Romney suffered the most in his rectal misery. His groans as the ship rolled were only matched by those of the *Michael* as her timbers worked in the violence of the storm.

We were taking on water.

On the second night we felt a great shock which tossed all us larbolins from our hammocks as we slept below decks. We scrambled up to find that we'd run aground on some reef in the dark. The boat was taking on water now to an alarming degree.

McPherson ordered that we should abandon ship.

Life jacketed and in the ship's boat we pulled for the storm washed unknown shore where all fell asleep, exhausted by the ordeal, right where we fell.

When we woke in the morning we saw the ship wrecked upon a shoal or reef a cable's length or two from the shore. She was a smashed hulk, waves crashing through her, the tide pulling her apart.

In all fairness, one member of the ship's company felt there was a silver lining to the ship's otherwise tragic loss. Romney discovered that spread upon the surface of the waters was a translucent, gelatinous layer of the very balm that would soothe his anal complaint. He hollowed out coconut halves and filled them with the stuff and ran into the forest, only to burst out moments later with a childish grin and, splashing into the surf, collect more for later.

In addition to rectal remedies, we took what we could from the *Michael* and from it built a makeshift shelter on the beach. About us were tropical forests, all asound with great buzzing insects and snakes and what-have-you.

Pearce, our expert castaway, promised that there should be wild boar on the island that we might catch.

Not that I'd be what you call picky under the circumstances, I said. But is the wild boar a well tasting beast, Mr. Pearce?

Oh, yes, he said. It is almost the choicest of meats. I would rate it the second most soylent I have ever tasted.

Soylent, you say? Booper asked.

Did I say soylent? How silly of me. I meant succulent. Succulent, he stressed.

That first night the rains quenched our fire and tormented us most terribly. I can't imagine many of us slept at all, though McPherson slept the sleep of the just in his best dress uniform upon the sand that night.

In the morning we rebuilt the shelter, this time with a roof.

As the days went on we struggled to find food and water, the boar having made themselves scarce, and in the nights we saw the central mountain of the island — a large mound like a great upturned bowl with two rounded peaks rising higher from either side — awash with the lights and thunderous booms of volcanic explosions. There were strange, unnatural noises coming from the jungle.

One early afternoon Alexander Pearce called a Castaway Council. He held a fistful of cut seagrasses.

Gentlemen, said he. The time of choosing is upon us. Soon we will have to eat whatever we can to survive. Sacrifices will have to be made.

Are you suggesting, I said. That we resort to cannibalism?

I am.

Egads, man! Shouted Romney. We've only been here four days!

I'm a planner, Pearce explained, somewhat cowed.

Well, Romney continued. We're not going to consider cannibalism on Thursday, when we only got here on Monday. For one thing there's still salt horse and biscuit left. Now, I'll have you know that Captain McPherson and I have convened a Committee on Rations, a Subcommittee on Liquid Rations and a Blue Ribbon Committee on Rescue. We have imbued these several bodies with subpoena power over both the ship's people and the several species of animals found upon this island, including those as yet undiscovered. The Committee on Rations meets twice weekly and every alternate Friday, which means, Pearce, that your concerns can come before the committee tomorrow as long as you submit your request to appear upon the agenda in writing by sundown tonight.

I just wanted to know when we can start considering cannibalism, that's all, Pearce said, staring down at a broken conch shell he was worrying with his foot.

McPherson intervened and busied us crew with various jobs: another attempt at fishing, some gathering of firewood, weaving a great awning out of palm leaves, Hoff was tasked with trying to make a working signal flare from the soused ones we'd recovered from the *Michael* and Pearce was set to the task of writing help on the beach in giant letters that might be seen by a passing airplane.

As the sky darkened that evening we all gathered at the shelter. Hoff showed us the signal flare he'd jury-rigged. We decided that the sky was dark enough to chance it so we all stood back as Hoff fired it off.

A great bursting flower in the sky, it was, coloring the night. We all went abed in hopes that we would soon be rescued.

How strangely were our prayers answered.

I think the burlap bag was over my head before I was ever awake. There were the voices of several women and a confusion of grunts, stumblings and warnings. Never before or since have I been subject to so many pokes with a nightstick.

Next thing I knew I was strapped to a chair

and a bright light shone in my face. The room felt like a bunker of some sort, all concrete and steel. The rest of the *Michael's* people were similarly bound.

Romney sat, bound to a folding chair as we all were. A blond woman stood over him, her flashlight lighting his terrified face.

You're here to cure your hemorrhoids, you say? she shouted at Romney.

That's not–it's complicated, a very flustered Romney said.

Was the gel mass floating just offshore complicated, sir?

Let it go, Agent Elsa! a clam-shell-brassiered woman with red hair shouted. Those are pearls that were his piles. This is a strange place for him, a whole new world!

Look, Booper interjected. I can explain.

All the flashlights spun to focus upon his blubbering gob.

It's a long story, he said.

Let's take these poor unfortunate souls to see the kommissar, said a dark, strikingly beautiful woman in flowing harem pants.

Agent Jasmine is right, Agent Elsa said.

We were marched to another chamber. In the hallway I heard someone behind me stumble. I turned to look.

Don't turn around! said a little man in a phrygian cap.

It was then that I noticed that there were

seven of them, little men in phrygian caps. They were called Slappy, Crappy, Hangry, Mangey, Dickey, Spiteful and Cock.

They swung their billy clubs indiscriminately. Agent Snow had her hands full trying to keep them in line.

We soon found ourselves in a grand stone chamber. At its head was a mighty plinth upon which sat a young woman. She was dressed in grasses.

Kommissar Moana! Agent Jasmine called. We bring to you the interlopers. Have you heard their story?

I have, Moana said. I find it hard to believe. Firstly, it introduces side characters — the intent here was clearly commercial; they have licensing potential — but then drops them with nary a word. The plot then continues willy-nilly—

Your honor, ma'am, Booper said. It's not as if our story included a Macguffin with previously unexplained powers to attract evil entities only to never mention this quality again after the antagonist in question is driven off.

Kommissar Moana narrowed her eyes.

I suppose the infraction could be forgiven, she said, if the source of all the trouble, which involved many, many people and caused untold destruction and ended with your unwelcome and unpaid-for stay here on Walt Disney's Happy Joy Perfection Paradise Resort Island, would resolve the conflict with an earnest apology.

That's ludicrous! Booper declared.

Is it? the kommissar said with a raised eyebrow.

You'd have us believe, for example, that an epic sequence of events spanning generations and causing entire cultures to abandon their exploratory way of life could be resolved with a simple apology.

Yes, she said.

At this Booper walked up to Romney and, holding his hat in his hands, said, Mr. Romney, I am very sorry for all the pain I have caused you.

I forgive you, Booper, Romney said.

As we were unbound, Kommissar Moana turned to Booper and said, You're welcome.

✱ ✱ ✱

The next day we were removed from the island and banned from all Disney properties for a year. Only Alexander Pearce chose to stay at the resort, where he has since risen to the role of Chief of Exotic Meat Procuration.

22nd March 2022

BOOPER MCCARTHY AND THE UNQUIET SHADE OF SALUBRITY PRESCOTT

Booper and I didn't even begin to feel safe until we were an hour south of Christchurch, speeding away from the livid mob through the darkness in Sam's truck, the last angry theater-goer spotted three quarters of an hour before. Booper was in the back with the sheep, but up against the cab — its rear window was open — so he could bless Sam and me with the inane blather that passed for his conversation.

I mean, Booper said. I was under no illusion that I'd written a second *Hamilton*, but I'd not considered the possibility that the audience would react so, so violently. I thought the Kiwis were kind, tolerant flightless bir —

People, you idjit, I interjected, half under my breath.

The truck struck a bump in the road. One of the sheep bleated in annoyance.

People, sorry, Booper said.

We are, Sam said. Now, Booper. Negative reviews are part of every artist's experience. It's almost a right of passage.

Particularly, I said, when the auteur in question once had a six-month case of hysterical blindness cured by a barber.

They bled him?

No — Jesus, Mary and Joseph! — they gave him a haircut.

Sam stifled a laugh.

That's as may be, he said. A disastrous production happens to everybody.

Even you, Sam? Booper asked, nay, pleaded.

Even — he considered a moment — well, I suppose, it happens to almost everybody.

✳ ✳ ✳

Perhaps, dear reader, I owe you an explanation as to how Booper and I got here in the first place.

To say that our stage production *Event*

Horizon: The Musical! was an unmitigated disaster would be an understatement of the same degree as calling Fat Man a firecracker. I should have seen that the whole project was cursed from the very beginning, being the brainchild of one Booper McCarthy, himself being blessed with neither children nor brain. The only positive decision he made was to premier the thing in Christchurch, New Zealand, though it was made in the desire that might fulfill his lifelong desire to see a toilet flush the other way. Had the show been seen by an audience in London or New York, Booper and I would be dead men.

After escaping the theater by way of a third-floor window, descending by means of a great length of prop viscera, we climbed into the bed of a livestock transportation truck packed with sheep, gathering that we had a remarkably diverse audience.

Eventually the truck pulled out of the lot and, with Booper and myself hiding face down underneath the mass of sheep, began to navigate its way out of the city.

At a quiet, stop-lit intersection the rear window of the cabin opened.

No worries, a pleasant voice said from within. I know you're there, I know who you are and I'll take you to safety.

We had no choice, I suppose, but to accept this.

I'm called Sam, by the by.

Or pleasure, entirely, I called from beneath a particularly amorous ewe *sotto voce* as the truck began to move again. I don't mean to impose, Sam, but would it be possible for me to join you in the cabin at the next intersection? I'm gaining an uncomfortable familiarity with your livestock, under the current conditions.

Certainly! he said.

It was when I'd climbed into the cab that I realized our rescuer was none other than star of screens both big and small, Sam Neill.

Booper, I said. Can I tell you something? Our savior is none other than star of film Sam Neill!

Ah, do you tell me so, Bryan? He's the star of me favorite film — what's it called? — the one with the dinosaurs.

Oh, ho, Sam chuckled. There were several.

I have it! Booper cried. *Fern Gully*!

All I could do at this brazen display of stupidity was bash the fore-part of my cranium upon the dashboard.

It's okay, Bryan, Sam said. I'm a lover of all film.

The truck grove on through the night.

I hope, I ventured, you were not offended by our little homage?

Not at all! Sam cried. Delightful! The kick line to "*Liberate Tutamet Ex Infernis*" was eye opening, to say the least. I'm shocked that you could find such a prodigious volume of artificial blood!

Hold it! Hold it, now, Booper said. Am I to understand — I a producer, writer, director and star of the musical in question — am I to understand that, upon the open market, one can find such a thing as *artificial* blood?

Ye gods, Sam gasped.

Now, Sam, I said loud enough to drown out any further protestations on either his or Booper's part. What did you think of the heart-rending ballad "We Won't Need Eyes To See"?

Musically? he said. Powerful. Though if you are to take the show on tour your actor-marionettes will certainly require on-tour chiropractic care.

You are most kind, I said. I will be sure to make a note of that. Many thanks to you.

You're very welcome, Sam said. As a career-long recipient of profoundly meaningful mentorship, I consider it a professional obligation. An obligation which I embrace whenever I can.

Thus did our discussion turn to the thoroughly negative reviews our show was certain to receive.

Thirst was a work, I said, for its time and place. To those at its heart it was drawn comedic tension. For outsiders I can imagine it being taken as subtly funny or it may even miss the mark entirely. But never did I imagine an audience so hating a work that I was to become, in their eyes, the human equivalent of an old timey public men's room piss-trench.

Sam's engine hummed along.

A sheep bleated.

Worse, if you think about it, Booper said. At least the piss-trench had a function.

Now, now, Sam interrupted. Out of the dumps, you two! I'm taking you to the most remote house in New Zealand. We've quite a drive, so let's talk about what you did well.

I liked the song "(Do We Need A) Gravity Drive," Booper said.

I'm a very quick study, Sam said, when it comes to music and lyrics. Do you mind if I have a go?

> *I created this ship to reach the stars*
> *But she's gone much, much too far*
> *She's torn a rift through time and space*
> *A path to Hell I can't erase*

Booper and I joined in:

> *Do we need a gravity drive?*
> *Or is the alternative stayin' alive?*
> *At least I wouldn't be here despisin'*
> *This ship they call Event Horizon*

Sam took the plaintive, falsetto coda for himself:

> *If I'd not made this gravity drive*
> *I'd not be on this ship*
> *That's*

Alive!

What a chorus we made! And for the first time since well before the show we laughed and laughed.

What do you think. Booper asked, about the number "The Lewis and Clark (This Ol' Tub)"?

Well, Sam said judiciously, I thought the song was great, but the imagery of Weir's wife in the tub was somewhat arresting. I will say that to rhyme the title of "The Forward Section" with vivisection was a stroke of genius.

Did you enjoy, Booper continued as if he'd not been heard, the overture I composed? It was performed entirely on vazooleyhorns.

Vazoo—?

Vuvuzelas, I helped.

Ah, yes, Sam said. I thought I recognized the caressing tones of the vuvuzela. So very sweet.

Our conversation died down and Sam drove through the night. Booper lay snoring in the truck bed having wrestled a ewe or two into performing the duty of a blanket.

This is no mere remote house I'm taking you to, Sam said. But the famed Prescott House.

I'm sorry to say, I said. I've never heard of it.

You won't be bothered by neighbors or any angry theater-goers, he said.

Good, I said. We'll be safe.

From them, Sam said. But I daresay you'll have to keep your wits about you.

We both peered at Booper, snuggled like a little lamb.

I suppose I'll have to be wits enough for the both of us.

Indeed. Booper. Is he brave?

Booper? Brave? Why, I'm convinced he's the only spatchcocked human alive.

Then you'll need to be backbone enough for the two of you, as well. The Prescott House is haunted. Some say doubly so.

Do you tell me so, Sam?

It all began in the mid-to-late 19th century with Doctor Prescott's Patented Nerve Tonic. Claimed he'd been led by an aborigine elder into an ancient, abandoned Vegemite mine where he'd discovered a miraculous curative made with a secret blend of brown booby guano and mother-of-Vegemite. Needless to say Prescott — Bernard Prescott, if memory serves — was no doctor and the ingredients in his nerve tonic were not nearly as wholesome as he claimed. He made millions before it was conclusively tied to thousands of deaths.

Saints preserve us!

Turns out the active ingredients were arsenic and lead. He was hanged by an angry mob and his body torn to pieces.

Horrible, horrible. But what does this have to do with his house?

Oddly enough, the house was never really

his. His wife, a lady called Salubrity Prescott, had just begun to build the house when the supposed doctor met his end. She was completely innocent in the despicable business, they said, but was tortured by what she claimed were the ghosts of those her husband's tonic had killed. She said they would never let her finish the house. So it's an eclectic maze of myriad architectural styles. Stairways to nowhere. Doors that open to precipitous multi-story drops.

This sounds just like the — what d'you call it? — Remington House! California, I think. Say, do these ghosts haunt the house still? Mrs. Prescott must be long dead by now.

No, Bryan, Sam said. Those ghosts do not; but hers does. She's an interesting ghost. Rather pleasant, in fact. But they say there's another ghost, one that haunts the Red Drawing Room. Second floor, I'm told. In the Empowerment Wing. They say it gets lovely light in the afternoon. But as to the horrors to be found in there, I know nothing.

I must have dozed off after that. When I awoke the sun was rising and the green hills of New Zealand were in their glory. It looked like paradise itself.

The house was a ramshackle affair, at once grandiose and rustic. Porticos and flying buttresses next to *Fallingwater*-esque natural geometry next to what might have passed for farm outbuildings the house had overtaken and incorporated. Sam dropped us at the front door

— unlocked! — and promised to check in on us tomorrow.

The entry to the house was an enormous atrium, three stories high. Into it from the second floor protruded a bathroom with clear glass floor, ceiling and wall. Even the toilet was glass.

I hope all the lavatories are not like that, I said.

That's how they are in the White House! Booper declared.

Now you're pulling my leg, Booper.

Hand on me heart it's true! Been that way since Taft got himself stuck in a bathtub. The way I see it, if it's good enough for the world's number one man to produce a number two in, it's good enough for Booper McCarthy!

We decided to split up: I to find a kitchen or pantry for some food; he to clean up and see if he could find something to wear that didn't smell like livestock.

It was strange to find fresh food in the house — I'd already resigned myself to a diet of spam, tuna fish and sardines — but I guess they must have a high standard for haunted houses in New Zealand. There was a fresh loaf of bread and cheeses and slicing sausages, including an excellent Ibérico de Bellota chorizo. I'd put together one of my famous charcuterie displays — I've been making them for years, long before doing so was either popular or profitable — when Booper came into the kitchen looking like an Edwardian gentleman, pipe and smoking jacket and all.

Booper, I said. Where did you find those togs? For the first time in your life entire you look respectable.

Thank you, Bryan! The magic voice said it would suit me.

The what you say?

He puffed at his pipe.

The magic voice. I went into the dressing room and the voice said, "Bernard?" "Yes," I said. "Your clothes are waiting for you." I had no idea what it was all about, but then she said, "You should wear the paisley smoking jacket." So here I am. The pipe was my idea.

Since when do you smoke a pipe, Booper?

He pulled out a pocket watch.

Approximately three and a half minutes ago, he said.

Bernard, said a woman's voice, deep, which seemed to originate and resonate from every direction within and without at once. Is this the Bryan you were telling me about?

Of course! Bryan, Magic Voice. Magic Voice, Bryan.

I took off my hat.

Delighted, ma'am, I said uncertainly.

But you know my name, Bernard, the voice said. We discussed it.

Yes! Booper said. Of course, Sobriety.

There was a quiet pause.

Legubrity?

Another pause, and this so pregnant I imagined we were expecting elephant triplets.

Booper, may I? I said. I believe her name is Salubrity.

That's right! The voice said with saccharine enthusiasm. You are capable of achieving our dreams!

See now, Booper, I said.

He just stood there slicing cheese, pretending he couldn't hear me.

Salubrity, I said with self-satisfaction.

Now, gentlemen, the voice said. There is something I need the two of you to take care of for me, if you can, in the Red Drawing Room.

I froze in panic.

Madam Prescott, I said. I'm not sure that's something we can do. We are mere men, after all.

Of course you can! The voice said. Envision the reality you want to achieve! You are omni-capable!

I gather you are not familiar with our work in the legitimate theater, I said. And I say that with all due respect.

Now, Bryan, that's all stuff, Booper said. We can certainly handle a room! It's like Julius Caesar said upon marching into Gaul: "Be the change you want to see in the world!"

That's the spirit, Bernard! the voice said.

Booper puffed smugly at his pipe.

Saw the play, I did, Booper said. Abbey Theater. Milo O'Shea himself played the great man.

As Booper reminisced, the disembodied voice of Salubrity Prescott guided us to the door of the Red Drawing Room.

The door stood open.

The demon came, she said, fifteen years ago. Since then my spirit has been unable to pass this threshold.

Booper cleared his throat.

Why don't you lead the way, Bryan? I'll make sure no hell-beasts try to surprise us from the rear.

The door slammed behind us once we had entered. The room was chill and silent. All red, it was, with a low ceiling and furnished with a neo-Edwardian meets shabby chic flair. There were uncomfortable looking chairs, a divan and, for reasons Booper and I could never make out, a four poster bed, fully curtained and looking like it had been made this morning.

I could sense that we were not alone.

Only my exhaustive reading of the Thomas Carnacki stories could save us now.

* * *

A week or so later, I held a dinner at my place in Number 4 Cheyne Walk. The usual company were there, Hodgeson, Jessop, McCarthy and, as a particular surprise, Ms. Carpenter. Tonight we were also joined by the esteemed Dr.

John Silence, of whose exploits I've no doubt you are all aware. My usual custom obtained: There was to be no attempt to draw me into discussion of my latest investigation until after dinner and we'd retired to my smoking room with our brandy.

I began.

As you know, Booper and I were investigating the Red Drawing Room Affair. A rather rare case, the like of which I've only ever seen in the Case of the Licari Infestations and the Ladies' Toilet Case, though it has some similarities to the various Goldstein Manifestations I've encountered. These, as you know, nearly cost me my life. The similarity will become more apparent when I publish my monograph *On the Complete and Unabridged Tablets of Gil-Ga-Mesh*.

Booper and I sat in the room until dark. He suggested we "smudge" the room — which, as you know, I think is all stuff — but I humored him and, using his livestock-stinking old socks — why he had them in the pockets of his smoking jacket I'll never know — I "smudged" in the corners of the room, ceiling and floor and around the windows and door.

And there we sat until midnight, Booper stretched out, somewhat awkwardly, on the divan and I perched uncomfortably in a chair I'd drawn into a corner so that I could have an unobstructed view of the room.

When the clock struck midnight — Jove! did I get the queerest feeling — I began to hear the springs flex in the bed behind the curtains.

Bryan, McCarthy whispered, there's something in the bed!

Before I could stop him he'd dived into the bed through the curtains.

I've got you now! he shouted in triumph, bouncing on the bed, curtains wrapped about him covering his eyes. Still he bounced until he'd braced himself with his hands upon the ceiling.

Bryan! Bryan! he cried. There are letters on the ceiling!

What are you about, man? I demanded, shining a flashlight where his hands were.

In the popcorn! he said. In the popcorn ceiling! Letters!

Can you make any of them out, bedam, Booper?

I can, Bryan, but they don't make any sense, unless it's some homophobic graffiti. It's in braille!

I got out a pen and some paper.

Spell it out for me, Booper, I said.

C-A-V-E-H-O-M-O-H-I-C-I-N-F-E-R-N-U-S-E-S-T, he said. And then another, a little lower. S-A-T a space and S-P-A-C. What d'you make of it, Bryan?

I ran to the door and threw it open.

Mrs. Prescott! I called. Mrs. Prescott!

Yes, Bryan, she said.

You said this room has been haunted for the last fifteen years. What happened in this room fifteen years ago?

Why, she said, I had the popcorn ceiling

done.

I smiled.

Mrs. Prescott, I said. We can get rid of your demon. All we need is Booper McCarthy's favorite appliance: a power washer.

Sam came by for breakfast next morning.

Fifteen years ago, I said, over freshly squeezed orange juice, Mrs. Prescott had the ceiling done by some fellows called Louie Sephir and Mephistophestephen from Satan's Spacklers.

That would be her first mistake, I'd imagine, Sam said.

Indeed, they wrote *"Cave Homo Hic Infernus Est"* into the popcorn of the ceiling.

In braille! Booper said with triumphant self-satisfaction.

"Beware, O man, this is hell" and that's all it took to bring on a demonic possession of the room, I said. Enough to make an archangel hold its breath. Just a little Latin in the ceiling spackle.

In braille! Booper said again.

In braille? Sam asked. See, I would have thought it would have been written in — here he gave a wry smile and a wink — cursive!

❋ ❋ ❋

I said good night to my dinner guests and had Blackwood show them out into the darkening evening on Cheyne Walk.

✽ ✽ ✽

Some time I should tell you about the time Booper and I met a man from Nantucket.

31st July 2022

WHERE WALDO WAS

It was shortly after Christmas in the year '20. Booper and I were in the office we shared at the Ordinary Times Investigative Bureau, Building Three, Third Floor. I was sitting at my desk admiring the very thoughtful Christmas gift I'd been given by Will Truman, a beautiful pistol, a Chekhov 1911. Booper was lounging in his gift, a hammock he'd managed with great difficulty to sling across the office and then, with even greater difficulty — looking like a particularly ungainly giraffe being taken by surprise by a net — mounted.

Nice of him to give you a gun, Booper said. What d'you suppose he imagined you doing with it?

Given that you are likely to cause yourself grievous bodily injury getting in and out of that hammock, said I, I imagine he pictured me putting you out of your misery.

Would you be a lad and do that for me

should the circumstance arise? he asked.

Of course! I said.

The intercom buzzed. It was my confidential secretary, Ms. Trollop.

Mr. O'Nolan, she said. The Wally Watchers are here to see you.

The who now?

The Who are not currently touring, Mr. O'Nolan, due to the pandemic.

Not those who, I said, the who that are here.

These who? The Wally Watchers.

Still beyond fuddled, I told her to send them in.

All my life, Booper McCarthy, I thought you were the one person I could speak to and the more questions I'd ask the less informed I'd be, and yet here we are, I said.

Here we are, he confirmed sagely.

In the Wally Watchers came, and what a strange set they were into the bargain. They all wore blue jeans; some had round Windsor-style glasses. All had at least one garment — a hat, a scarf or a shirt — in red and white hoops. They could only crowd halfway into the room — what with Booper's hammock stretched across — so they piled in and stood awkwardly up against it while Booper gazed up at them, smiling benevolently like an expectant child.

Are you in some sort of show? I asked, trying not to come across as condescending.

No, one of them said eventually, having

wordlessly consulted his fellows.

Are you some sort of traveling troupe or band?

Not exactly, another one said.

Well, what are you?

We're the Wally Watchers! a third volunteered enthusiastically.

That isn't very helpful. What is it that you Wally Watchers do?

We watch Wally! they said.

I put my face in my hands.

Now, Bryan, Booper said. Even I could see that coming.

I took a deep breath.

And who is this Wally that you watch?

Well, said one. Wally, or Waldo, is a world traveler and time travel enthusiast!

Do you tell me so, in point of fact?

We watch him all the time, wherever he goes! said another. Waldo is known for his distinctive mode of dress.

The entire group of Watchers showed off their outfits.

So I see. And how can the crack investigative team of Booper and I be of assistance?

We've lost him! He's disappeared! We haven't seen him for days! they all seemed to shout at once.

No updates to his social media!

No activity on his credit cards!

We found no evidence in our weekly sift of

his garbage!

We need to know: Where's Waldo?

I think if I were this Waldo, I might want to disappear myself, I muttered.

No, no. This is very unlike him, they said. The only clue we've found are these.

They proffered a pair of glasses — reaching awkwardly across the gently swinging form of Booper McCarthy — in the very style the Watchers themselves wore.

Please, Mr. O'Nolan, they pleaded.

Alright, fine. I'll find him. But if the man just wants to be left alone in peace, alone in peace he shall be left.

They nodded enthusiastically.

Now, where did you find these spectacles?

In a shoe store, one said. On top of one of those...things.

Things?

You know, she said. Those do-hickeys.

No, no, said another. It's more of a gizmo.

You know, said a third, those metal dealies you use to measure your feet in a shoe store.

Ah, a Brannock Device! I said triumphantly.

A what? said Booper with such force he nearly threw himself out of the hammock.

A Brannock Device, you great clod! The device you use to measure your show size. And now I know just where to start. Do you still have that all terrain food truck, Booper? I suspect we're going to need it.

Well, Andrew Donaldson took my keys, but I'm fairly certain he gave them to Ms. Trollop.

In half an hour I had successfully extricated Booper from the hammock — managing to do so harming neither Booper nor the hammock — and we were gassed up and on our way to Liverpool, New York: home of the Brannock Device.

❊ ❊ ❊

Now, if you've ever been to Liverpool, New York in the winter, you know it as a lonely, snow-packed canal stop whose chief contributions to the world — other than the Brannock Device — are Seasonal Affective Disorder and small, hypertension-inducing salty potatoes — Jesus, Mary and Joseph does Booper enjoy the salty potatoes — and separated by a lake equal parts Mercury and wastewater from the Mordor of Upstate, Syracuse.

Thankfully, Booper had thought to mount the cow catcher attachment to the front of the food truck. It functioned as a passable plow as we wandered the serotonin-depleted streets.

We searched in vain for a show store in hopes that someone could direct us to the Brannock World Headquarters; the closest thing we could find was a haberdashery by the library called Handford's.

We plowed ourselves a parking spot and

went in.

I was immediately discouraged; the shop was full of hats. Not a shoe in sight. But then I saw something that told me that we were in the right place: The woman behind the counter was dressed in bluejeans, a red and white hooped shirt and hat and heavy-rimmed glasses.

Top of the mornin' to you, ma'am, I said.

Welcome to Handford's! My name is Wilma. How can I help you?

We're looking for a man who lost these glasses, I said, handing the spectacles in question to her. He has a group of hangers-on who are concerned for him.

She recognized the glasses instantly.

Waldo! These are Waldo's!

I turned from the desk to call to Booper, who was browsing straw hats at the front of the store.

Do you hear that, Booper? We're on the right track, begob!

I turned back to the clerk, who stood scrutinizing the glasses.

Now, Wilma, that's —

Wilma? she said with a laugh. I'm Wenda!

I'm sorry, what?

Wenda, she said. Wilma's identical twin sister.

Ah! I turned to Booper again. Twins, to beat the band. How silly of me. Twins! Well, I said, turning back to Wenda, my apologies, Ms. Wenda.

Wenda? No, I'm Wilma! she said.

I jumped to the counter to see where Wenda had gone.

It's okay, she said. We find ourselves suddenly switched without explanation. We're not sure if it's due to a continuity error or a typo.

Do you tell me so? An error of the continuity. How very strange.

It has its benefits. We're able to draw double pay, appearance fees, royalties, all without ever having to appear at the same time.

Well, I said, if there must be injustice in the world, you've at least managed to turn it to your own advantage.

I wasn't sure how to feel about this, I don't mind telling you.

Regarding the owner of these spectacles, I said.

Oh, yes! Waldo. I suspect his nemesis, Odlaw, is behind this.

Tell me more about this Odlaw, if you please.

Well, he looks just like Waldo, except his clothes are yellow and black, he wears blue-tinted glasses and has a mustache. His bad deeds are many.

What sort of bad deeds are they? I asked.

Many.

I looked quizzically at her.

Look, she said, it's a picture book. There's limited exposition.

Fair play, fair play, I said. Is there anything else you can tell me about this nefarious nemesis?

Well, she thought for a moment. He's always after Waldo's magical cane. You should consult Wizard Whitebeard, he knows all about this sort of thing.

Being magical, I allowed.

Being magical. Right, she said. He lives in a yurt in Hanford, Iowa.

Did you say Handford? Like this haberdashery?

No, Hanford.

So there's Handford's Haberdashery...

Yes.

And Hanford, Iowa.

Umhm.

Seems coincidental.

Does it? Would you prefer Hanford, Washington? That one's radioactive.

Iowa, it is, then, I said. Thank you for your help, Wil—

Wenda! Booper called. Oh, and Bryan. One more thing before we leave.

* * *

Sixteen hours west down Interstates 90 and 80, Booper and I — bedecked in our new straw hats — arrived at Wizard Whitebeard's yurt in Hanford, Iowa.

Booper, I said as I shut down the engine of his food truck, I confess I am entirely ignorant regarding the, shall we say, etiquette one ought to employ in addressing a yurt and its dweller.

Yurtiquette? Booper said. Leave it to me; I once ate the Mongolian Barbecue.

Once ate the Mongolian Barbecue? Since when does that confer expertise in—

Bryan, I was in Ulaanbaatar, formerly known as Niïslel Khüree. It has been Mongolia's principal city for centuries.

And?

The cuisine was delicious.

Before I could stop him, he was standing, arms wide, calling to the yurt:

O, yurt! And dweller within, I summon thee in friendship!

Out from the yurt came a tall man in a red robe and a pointy blue hat. A ponderous long beard had he and a red scarf lay upon it.

Behold, he said, adopting the same stance as Booper. I am Wizard Whitebeard and I am he who dwells within this yurt. Greetings!

Greetings! Booper replied.

Wizard Whitebeard eyed the side of Booper's truck.

You come bearing victuals, I see! I will have a dozen of your Painful Anus Wings and a side order of Potato Toddlers.

Booper and I fumbled, at a loss for words.

Oh, he said. With chipotle mustard and a

lemonade.

Sir, Mr. Wizard Whitebeard, I began—

No need for formality, friend, he said. You may simply call me Wizard Whitebeard.

Wizard Whitebeard. Yes. Unfortunately, this food truck is no longer a going concern and has been reduced to a mere conveyance — he looked crestfallen — We have come to you in search of a man you know.

I've not had Potato Toddlers for many years. How disappointing. Good thing I've got feuchtwangers of my own in the fridge.

No more disappointed than we are, let me assure you, I said. We are here, shall I say—

On a quest! interjected Booper.

On a quest to find Waldo.

Wally is missing? asked Wizard Whitebeard, aghast.

Yes. Question: Why is he sometimes Wally and other times Waldo?

Localization, he said. In some regions he's Wally; in others, Waldo.

Fascinating! said Booper, in awe.

Indeed. In France, he's Charlie. In Israel, he's Efi and in Turkey he's Gezgin Veli.

Must create a difficult passport situation, I said. Inconvenient for a world traveler and time travel enthusiast.

That's where his magic walking stick comes in handy.

Is this the same magic walking stick that

Wilma and, or Wenda told us about? The one that Odlaw has tried to steal?

The very same.

Wenda and, or Wilma suggested that Odlaw might be behind Waldo's disappearance.

Yes, Wizard Whitebeard said. Odlaw's bad deeds are many.

So we've heard. Might you know where Waldo may have gone?

Yes, he said. I sent him on a quest of self-discovery. To New York City in September of 1922.

Drat, I said. This is the end of the line, then. The truck can do much, but certainly not travel through time.

I can help you with that, but it is not without peril. I will send you to find him. If you can find Waldo or his walking stick, you will be transported back here. What is today?

January the fourth.

January the fourth. But, if you cannot the man or his walking stick, you will be stranded in the past for the rest of your lives.

It's a deal! Booper said, before I could express my misgivings.

Gentlemen, he said. Into the truck.

Booper dragged me inside as Wizard Whitebeard began his incantation:

> *Higgledy-pig*
> *Art deco design*
> *I transport this food truck*
> *Back in time!*

There was a swirl of color and a great crashing noise as Booper and I were thrown bodily to the floor of the cooking compartment. We stood, brushed ourselves off and straightened our straw hats.

A time traveling food truck, I muttered. Ludicrous, just ludicrous. It strains credulity more than those books you made me read to you about the time traveling librarian.

Someone knocked on the outside of the truck. It sounded like there was a great commotion going on out there.

Now look here, I said, opening the service window. Mr. Wizard—

But the man who gazed up at me was not Wizard Whitebeard, but a youngish man in a suit with a broad smile and a straw hat the spit of ours. What's more, we were parked on a city street!

Why, you are open! the man said. Well, ain't that the cat's meow. How many clams for an order of Potato Toddlers, Jackson?

I'm sorry, I said. But we're not currently open for business.

Applesauce, I'm starving!

From across the broad avenue, a gang of street toughs pointed at us and yelled.

The man pleaded to be let into the truck.

Can ya help a brother out, Jackson? They got a couple of big sixes and if we don't get a wiggle on there's going to be trouble.

We pulled him in and sped off.

What the hell is going on? I demanded.

There's a riot goin' on is what, Jackson. Anyone seen wearin' a straw hat after Felt Hat Day is liable to get bumped off, if those bluenosed Mrs. Grundys from Mulberry Bend are around.

Felt Hat Day?

Ya hoid right. September the fifteenth. The last day it's socially acceptable for a fella to wear a straw hat.

And there's a riot going on to enforce this rule?

You got it, bub.

Is there anywhere that's safe?

Sure, I know a speakeasy 'round the corner.

Once ensconced in the bar, we showed our new friend — his name is O'Reilly — Waldo's glasses.

Sorry. I don't recognize these cheaters, he said. But there's this hard-boiled private dick comes 'round this place. Name of McGillicuddy. Lemme see if he's in.

I like the sound of this McGillicuddy, Booper said.

Do you now?

I'm confident in a man named McGillicuddy, he said. You can tell a lot from a man's name. McGillicuddy.

Do you tell me so, Booper McCarthy?

I do. McGillicuddy. Besides, he is a hard-boiled private dick after all.

And what, pray tell, is a hard-boiled private

dick?

Bryan, he said with a smile that filled his enormous, square head, I have no idea.

Just then O'Reilly returned, apologetic.

I'm sorry, he said. I found him, but he's spifflicated.

I'm sorry?
Canned?
No, not that.
Corked?
I don't folla.
Primed?
Afraid not.
Scrooched?
I'm at a loss.
Jazzed?
Not — no.
Zazzled?
Sounds exciting?
Owled?
No idea.
Embalmed?
Doesn't ring a bell.
Potted?
Nor that.
Ossified?
Drawing a blank, sorry.
Fried to the hat?
Booper and I just stared in utter confusion.
Drunk. He's drunk.
We know that one! we cried.

Well, he may have sobered up by now, he said. Still, I ain't makin' any promises.

McGillicuddy was drunk indeed. His straw hat was perched askance on the back of his crown. His hair was tousled and his eyes were glassy. His suit was disheveled. He stank of gin.

Wha'd'ya want? he growled, seeming to challenge the entire room.

We described Waldo and showed him the glasses.

Yeah, I seen 'im. He was tied up in the struggle-buggy of a hayburner driven by some egg wearing black and yellow. Left this behind.

He dropped an intricately carved ivory-colored walking stick onto the table.

Booper and I exchanged a wide-eyed glance.

Is that scrimshaw? I ventured.

McGillicuddy shrugged.

May I take a closer look?

I reached out for the walking stick.

The moment I touched the thing there was a swirl of color and a bang and we found ourselves back in the food truck.

Booper burst out into the January Iowa sunlight.

It worked! he declared, pulling Wizard Whitebeard into a hug. It worked! We found it!

It worked? Well, I'll be damned.

I brought out the carved walking stick.

It's scrimshaw, I think, which means there's only one man to consult. America's foremost amateur expert on scrimshaw art: Vice President Michael Pence.

* * *

Two days later we were at the Capitol Building in Washington, D.C.

As Michael's unofficial biographer, I not only have access to the super-secret parking garage, but I am also able to carry firearms, like the Chekhov 1911 Mr. Truman had given me a week prior, in the halls of Congress. Still, once we made it to the Capitol proper, we found people everywhere. Several times we thought we spotted Waldo when, in fact, we'd just spotted the stars and stripes in flag or garment form.

There were people milling about. In some places they were shouting or cheering. I'd never seen so unruly a mob in the Capitol.

We made our way to the underground Command Center.

The room was very tense and noisy. There were staffers running around and loosely controlled chaos to beat the band. We ran up to Michael.

Michael, I said, I'm so glad we've found you. We need a consultation. To make a long story short — I can see that you're busy — missing person. Questioned a wizard. Need you to identify some scrimshaw.

A wizard, you say? Michael said, grabbing my arm. He didn't, perhaps, resemble a shaman, did he?

Oh, no, I said. He was a wizard, pointy hat and long beard and all.

Ah, I see, said he. I'm sorry. I have much on my mind.

Of course, of course, Michael. I understand. Feast of the Epiphany, today. Always leaves one contemplating the higher things. Gifts of the Holy Ghost and such. Beautiful Mass at the Basilica this morning.

Sadly my mind is taken up with worldly, but gravely consequential concerns, Bryan.

An aide interrupted:

He refuses to answer on any line, sir.

Thank you, Ms. Harpootlian. Connie? he called to another aide. I'll put the finishing touches on that letter in just a moment.

Now, Michael, I said. I'll ask for the intercession of St. Sebastian that the Most High grant you strength and perseverance, that you may withstand the slings and arrows of outrageous fortune.

He was tied to a tree and shot with arrows, this Sebastian, Booper said.

That strikes home, Booper. These days it seems being tied to a tree and pierced by arrows is my vocation.

But he lived! Booper said. Thus the strength and perseverance and such.

Did he now? Michael said. That warms my heart, Booper. I can identify with this Sebastian of yours. Bryan, you've the gift of gab. What's the word for being trussed up to a tree and peppered with arrows for sport? Is there a word for that?

I considered.

I've got one! Booper said. Bullshit.

Michael smiled.

Connie, he called. I've found the right word for my sentiments in that letter: Bullshit.

The command center went quiet.

Sir?

You heard me, Michael said, smiling at Booper and me. Bullshit. Send the letter. Now, Bryan, let's see this scrimshaw you were telling me about.

We showed it to him.

Remarkable work! he said. Late eighteenth, early nineteenth century. Exquisite! Downeast, Maine or my name's not Michael Atticus Pence! If you'd know more, consult the good folks on Islesboro, Maine at the Alice L. Pendleton Museum.

Thank you, Michael!

You're most welcome. And Bryan, thank you for telling me about this Sebastian fellow. He will be my North Star in these trying times.

Booper and I winced.

What is it?

You should know, Michael, that after recovering from the arrows he harangued the Emperor Diocletian — speaking truth to power, if you will — and was cudgeled to death for it.

Michael was gobsmacked.

※ ※ ※

The next day we were in Belfast, Maine searching for information and a boat to Islesboro. After circling for over an hour I'd had enough.

Booper, I said. Pull over here; I need a coffee.

Fine, said he. I'll see what I can learn from this information kiosk.

When I returned, Booper was interrogating the kiosk attendant regarding what she knew about Napoleonic Wars era regional scrimshaw art. The poor young lady was cowering, tearful, trying to get Booper to accept tourism pamphlets.

Needless to say he was uninterested in puffin tours.

Booper, ya mad idjit, leave her alone! I shouted, but then I noticed something strange emerging from behind the kiosk.

It was a small dog with a red and white hooped sweater and hat and spectacle-shaped lines around his eyes. He was pulling a pair of bluejeans with his teeth.

Booper! I called. Look what I've found!

He rushed over.

I grabbed the bluejeans and tried to wrestle them from the dog.

Aww, what's your name, boy? I crooned.

Woof! The dog said.

Who's a good boy? I said, trying to calm him.

Woof! said the dog again.

Who's a sweet puppy?

The dog sat back on his haunches, letting the pants fall loose from his mouth.

Look, pal, he said. You asked my name and I answered you. I'm Woof.

Egads! cried Booper. A talking dog!

Booper, I said, folding my arms. In the last week you traveled to the 1920s, met a wizard and inspired Mike Pence to curse and this is where you refuse to suspend disbelief?

Fair enough, said he. Where's your master, boy?

Don't patronize me, hombre, Woof said. He's been kidnapped by Odlaw. I've tracked him this far and I suspect we should investigate the wharf.

Given that this was the closest thing to a solid lead we'd had throughout this entire investigation, we agreed.

We spotted that nefarious scofflaw trying to get into a skiff with an outboard motor, but Booper was too quick for him and held him fast.

Where's Waldo? I demanded.

I'll never talk, fed! Odlaw shouted defiantly.

I pulled the Chekhov 1911 from my waistband and leveled it at his heart.

Where's Waldo? I asked again.

Waldo, he muttered, despondent.

Exactly. Where's Waldo? Don't make me ask you again.

I told you. He's north of here. Up the river. In Waldo.

Waldo?

Yes, Odlaw said. In the Town of Waldo, in Waldo County, Maine.

Oh, I said. Well. I suppose I should have seen that coming. Take us to him!

He took us by boat up the Passagassawakeag into Waldo, Waldo, Maine and docked at a quiet jetty just as the dusk was closing in.

He opened the door to a little cabin and there was Waldo, hog-tied with his sweater and naked as the day he was born but for his red and white striped hat.

As Booper, Woof and I entered the cabin to untie him, Odlaw cackled and ran for the boat. I pointed my gun at him and pulled the trigger. Out came a nine-inch plastic shaft from which unfurled a pennant that said, "Bang."

Waldo was unharmed.

* * *

Sometime I should regale you with the tale of Mike's first colonoscopy.

22nd July, 2022

MIKE'S FIRST FORAY INTO POLITICS

This story is entirely fictional. To our knowledge, the real Mike Pence has never had any run-ins with Augustus Cobbledick.

Given that there is a heated presidential primary breaking out, many people have contacted me and asked how my good friend Mike Pence got into politics; the story is a good one.

It all started with a call from Booper. He'd been arrested, for neither the first nor last time, for attempting to scale the outside of a women's dormitory in an attempt to gain entry by way of upper floor windows. His one phone call, as always, was to Mike, who picked me up in his woody van on his way to the jail.

We bailed him out, of course, and put his dejected self in the back of the woody.

Booper, Michael said, I will never

understand why you keep climbing up these buildings!

Well, Booper said, with shame in his voice. I like fracking.

Booper, Mike said, what in the H-E-Charles-Kuralt does the extraction of our precious natural resources have to do with climbing up the outside of women's dormitories at night?

Ha! I never thought of it as a natural resource, Booper said, brightening.

Michael, I said, he's not talking about the fracking. He's all mixed up. Not right in the head. That's not what he means.

Well, what does he mean?

Hauley-pully? Booper offered.

What?

Amorous conversation? I said.

I still fail to understand you fellows, Michael said, with a note of exasperation in his voice.

Michael, he's referring to the — one could say — conjugal act, I said.

The van came to a screeching halt on the shoulder of the road.

I will not have such things discussed in the sacred confines of my woody, Michael declared. This is a place of reasoned discourse, honest discussion and occasional G-rated hijinks, it's not some bawdy van of ill repute!

We three fell silent, Mike fuming and Booper and I to varying degrees ashamed.

MIKE'S FIRST FORAY INTO POLITICS

I'm sorry, Michael, I do feel very low about all of this. Very low, Booper said.

I was exasperated. I'd had enough of Booper and his thoughtless schemes, the every one of which devolved into some escapade to rescue him from the consequences of his actions.

Ah, go piss up a drainpipe, ya idjit, I muttered.

I did, Booper said.

You did what? I said.

Piss up a drainpipe. I was three floors up when nature called. I didn't have much choice in the matter.

So you wet 'em? I said, aghast.

I did and I did and I not only wet 'em, Booper said in a sad, embarrassed puppy voice, there was other unpleasantness.

Well, Michael said. That would explain the smell.

I do feel very low, Booper said. Never lower, Michael. I am very sorry. Very, very sorry.

Sounds like you're the Mayor of Buck Town, Booper, Mike said.

The what of the what now? Booper asked.

Where I'm from, Booper, Mike said, when you're at your lowest low and you feel like you're down to your last buck, we say you're in Buck Town.

Oh, I am in Buck Town, Booper said. Maybe not mayor. Registrar for prostate, maybe. At best.

Boo— I began.

Just leave it, Bryan, Michael said. I have an idea that may benefit us all. Let's get out of Old Indy for a while and cool our heels somewhere more serene. Am I correct that you both have passports that are current? I'm thinking we should visit my ancestral summer home on Île Grande Miquelon.

Well, Booper began.

I interrupted.

Summer home? On an island, Michael? Do you tell me so?

I do, Mike said. I am, on the distaff side, descended from a long, proud, hearty line of Basque fishermen.

Basque fishermen? Booper said. But I thought you abhorred the whale fishery!

I have no idea what you are talking about, Booper, Mike said, putting the woody into gear and turning on his indicator to merge cautiously with the non-existent traffic.

Booper McCarthy, you're an idjit of gargantuan proportions! I said. He said Basque, not beluga.

Oh, ha ha! said Booper. Am I stupid!

Anyhow, Michael, I said, is that how you came to be fluent in the Basque?

Indeed, Bryan. *Nire lagunak oso ergelak dira, baina maite ditut*! But what of your passports?

Michael, Booper said, there was a series of unfortunate — if humorous — circumstances the result of which was that me passport and I were, shall I say, legally separated.

Ah, that is understandable, Booper, Micheal said. More understandable than you may appreciate. Thankfully, I've another plan in my head that we may find even more profitable.

Thus, Michael, instead, drove us to Stinesville, the smallest town in Indiana.

But why Stinesville, Michael? I asked.

Well, friend, he said, there's an election there for mayor, and it is so far uncontested. I thought I'd try my hand at politics and throw my hat into the race.

No, Michael, I said, no. You can't do that! Politics? A man that you know and that I know, one Booper McCarthy by name, is the very picture of the typical American voter!

I? Booper said. The typical American voter? Do you really mean that, Bryan?

I do, I said, nodding.

Why, I'm touched, Bryan, I truly am.

Michael and I exchanged looks.

Well, what issues are important to you? Mike asked, clearing his throat and turning to Booper.

Booper screwed up his face.

I don't folla, he said.

Mike searched for another way to crack the nut.

Are you a member of a political party? he asked.

Why, yes, the Sinn Féin, of course, Booper

said.

Mike smiled, thinking he was getting somewhere, no doubt.

So what draws you to Sinn Féin, Booper?

Why, me da was a member. And his da before him. And you know me love of the fireworks, of course.

That is well known, Mike said, his eyes clouding again.

Fireworks? Booper those were acts of terrorism!

They were? I don't folla the news, as you know. I hereby renounce the Sinn Féin! Booper said. That was a close one, Michael.

Booper, I prompted, tell him about the voting.

Oh, the voting! I'm a great man for the voting. Never miss an election. I'll tell you what I did the last time 'round, I will. I got me ballot and stood there in your man the booth with his nibs the curtain drawn behind and me black marker in me hand just like the proper voter and wouldn't you know it I couldn't decide! They all the candidates had such lovely sounding names, they did. I tell you what I did, I voted for alla them. I did, indeed! I took me black marker and I filled in alla the circles. Now, some of your men the candidates were outside the polling station and I said to them, I said, "Never fear, you got at least one vote! Booper McCarthy voted for you each and all!" Why, I enjoyed meself so much I went back later in the day to do it again. But the lady with the cards she says, "Now you listen here, Mr. Booper McCarthy," waggin' her finger in me face, she was, "You can only vote the once!" "Well," says I, "What a preposterous system. Elections only come 'round so often! All I was tryin' ta do is exercise me franchise." But she insisted, she did. Even had a constable come over to explain the thing! "Booper McCarthy," said he, "I'll have to take you to jail, I will, if you vote more than the once. I'd hate ta see ya in prison!" Well, I don't want that, neither, no sir. Most disappointing, the whole situation. Me very crest was fallen.

This, Michael, said I, is your man the voter.

Now, Bryan, said he, I'll not join you in so low an opinion of our fellow men as all that!

Fair enough, fair enough, I said, but you'll need skilled help if you're to campaign for public office, Michael. I suggest that our man Booper and I would be just the help you need to get you across the proverbial finish line.

Thank you, Bryan, Mike said. I appreciate the help, of course, but I am unfamiliar with any proverbs about crossing finish line.

Not proverbial, then, I said. I meant metaphorical. It was metaphorically proverbial in a non-literal way, tangentially speaking.

Bryan, how many of those words do you know the definition of?

I gave the question great consideration.

Why, several on their own and others in

company, I said.

Luckily for me, at this point we had arrived in the scenic little burg of Stinesville, Indiana.

Our first job is to size up the competition, Mike said, pulling into a driveway. In the middle of it sat, in a tired lawn chair, a grizzled man with a beard, a can of beer in his left hand and a shotgun resting in his lap. He was smoking a dilapidated cigarette.

Hello there, fellow hoosier! Mike said. I'm a new resident of Stinesville. I'm educating myself about the candidates — or candidate, as it may be— for mayor of this our fair city. Are you, in fact, Augustus "Scooter" Cobbledick?

Who's askin'? the man said with a scowl.

Well, I am Michael Pence and I'm considering a run for mayor.

The man grunted.

What's your platform, friend? Mike asked.

I just want to be left the hell alone, Scooter growled, the cigarette wagging like the tail of an excited terrier as he spoke.

Booper elbowed me.

You don't think, he said to me sotto voce, that this customer is one of them marijuana smokin' — what d'ya call 'em? — libraratarians, what with their antiquated notions of civil liberties and the objections to your men in the Bureau of the Alcohol, the Tobacca and the Firearms engagin' in routine animal control and search warrant operations? Your man Scooter is probably full of the alcohol, the tobacca and the firearms as we speak.

Now, Booper McCarthy, said I, why are you so afraid of your men the libertarians?

The libertarians? he said. The men that you know and that I know with their occupational licensing reform and their non-aggression principle? They'd kill ya as soon as look at ya, they would.

Kill? I said. Non-aggressively, I presume?

Alright, alright, Booper said. Passive-aggressively. The point is they'd kill ya for so much as lookin' at 'em.

Finished with his interview with Mr. Cobbedick, Mike led us back to the woody.

I think we should split up, he said. Why don't you two print up some signs and place them around town chatting up any locals you come by, while I go and register at City Hall and canvass the neighborhood.

That we did, and we met back at City Hall that evening for the debate, which was to be followed by the vote itself.

We found Mike at the back of the auditorium. There were three podiums — podia? — on the stage. Behind one stood Scooter Cobbledick. Behind another stood a man in tweeds and plus fours wearing a bowler hat.

Michael, I asked, eyeing the man suspiciously. That fella at the podium. Who's he when he's at home?

Oh, him? Mike said. He's a surprise development. This is now a three-man race, my friends. That man's name is Chaloner Ogle.

Ogle! What a lovely surname, Booper tittered.

How did the canvassing go, gentlemen?

Well, I met a man who was very concerned about the crop circles, I said.

And what did you tell him?

I told him you'd have the police department investigate.

Okay, Mike said, seeming somewhat perturbed. And you, Booper?

I had signs printed up, Booper said, but what I did is, I had them printed backwards and I put them on the wrong side of the road, so that when motorists see them in their rear view mirrors they'll read, "Michael Pence for Mayor. Take Stinesville in a new direction!" The printer asked did you intended to make everyone drive on the other side of the road. Now, Michael, I'll admit I'm not always nimble on me feet. I hadn't thought of such a thing! But it seemed like such a grand idea, I gave an enthusiastic affirmative and said you would!

Mike looked upset.

Would you have preferred "Mike" instead of "Michael"?

No, Booper, I'm in a bind. I don't know that I can get elected on a platform of driving on the left and extraterrestrial investigations.

Whatever will you do? I asked.

There's only one thing to do, gentleman. I must follow the Politician's Creed.

And how does that go, Michael?

"I am a politician," he recited, his right hand upon his heart, his eyes fixed in the middle distance. "I shall be at all times honest, accountable, transparent and forthright; I shall serve my constituents faithfully and to the best of my ability; I shall serve only so long as I am of use to the voters; I shall never engage in crass self-promotion, nor shall I seek the attention of the press for my own benefit; I will never seek to profit financially from the sacred position the voters might grant me the honor to serve them in. I am a politician."

Powerful stuff, Michael, I said.

This is no small favor I ask of the voters, Bryan. It is a calling.

They announced his name over the loudspeaker and he strode up to his podium for the debate like he was Seneca himself.

The moderator began.

Mr. Cobbledick, he said, how would you like to be left?

The hell alone, Cobbledick said, leaning into the microphone.

Mr. Ogle, the next question is yours. What are your first priorities, should you be elected mayor?

Crikey, guv! I 'spose it'd be better workin'

hours for the chiminey sweeps an' a cap on cab fares.

Hey! Someone shouted at the back. He's English!

Ogle looked panicked.

Mr. Ogle, are you or are you not in fact an American citizen? the moderator pressed.

Ogle put his face in his hands.

I ain't, sir. I ain't no such thing, he said and he ran off the stage.

Mr. Pence, is it true that you intend to have drivers in town travel on the left-hand side?

While that was not my intention, I am ultimately responsible for the promises made on my behalf by my campaign.

Is that a yes, Mr. Pence? the moderator asked.

Yes, Michael said. It is.

As for the police investigations—

Mike went to speak, but the moderator went on.

—Are you aware that the entirety of our police force is a retired malinois named Jan Vennegoor of Hesselink?

He played for Celtic! Booper gasped.

I, Mike began, I was not.

The audience was dismayed and there was a call for the voting to begin. After the votes were tallied, Mike, Booper and I joined Chaloner Ogle, sitting dejectedly on the curb outside town hall. All the votes but four had gone to Cobbledick. Mike and Ogle had split the remaining votes evenly.

I feel very low, Mike said. The only election I've won is to be the mayor of Buck Town.

Buck Town? Olge said.

Yes, said Mike. Where I'm from, when you're at your lowest low and you feel like you're down to your last buck, we say you're in Buck Town.

We sat silently, listening to Scooter Cobbledick's supporters cheering and firing guns into the night sky.

I thought you were going to win, Chaloner, Booper said. Such a lovely surname: Ogle.

Ogle whimpered.

I guess I'm feeling rather low myself, chums, he said.

Well, my British friend, Mike said, clapping a hand onto his shoulder. It sounds to me like you might just be the next mayor of Pound Town.

25th November 2022

THE TIME BOOPER & I LOST THE PENCE CHILDREN AT THE COUNTY FAIR

Looking back at his life it would seem absurd to let a confirmed fool — a man whose very name is a by-word for rank buffoonery — babysit one's children. But I am speaking of Booper McCarthy — so lovable a fool; we are not to see the like of him again — and so trusting were Mr. and Mrs. Michael Pence that, when they went on their annual autumn weekend excursion to Branson, Missouri they allowed himself and me to do just that.

I remember very well the discomfort on

display when Mr. and Mrs. Michael came home, herself as beautiful as always and himself in his finest Branson Suit, which consisted of a white-fringed black cowboy suit, a white ten gallon hat and a pink cravat.

Booper and I gathered the children, lately bathed and dressed and lined up at the landing of the foyer stairs all Von Trapp family fashion and ready for the presentation.

Michael and his lovely wife entered and the children beamed and all seemed well until Michael spoke to them.

How was your weekend, children? he asked.

I getted to hug the Yak Lady! said the youngest, Iphigenia, with great enthusiasm.

I made people throw up on the Cyclone ride! said Tanit, the middle child.

When I grow up, I want to live with the carnival folk! pronounced Marmaduke, the eldest, though still in his short pants.

There was a great silence in the entryway.

Bryan, Michael said, taking off his hat and clearly calming himself with herculean effort. Please explain.

And so explain I did.

* * *

It all began when I arrived at the Pence home. I was given all the typical instructions on what they the children should eat, what they could and could not watch on the television — no *Dukes of Hazzard*, under any circumstances — and which of Pastor Dennis's sermons was next in their listening schedule. If I recall it was the one entitled "God's Plan Regarding Municipal Light Railways." I wasn't paying attention to the whole four-and-a-half hours but I'm pretty sure He was in favor of them, as long as the fares were reasonable and they ran at decent hours of the day.

Again I digress.

To make a long story short, Booper showed up somewhat later — it was after Michael and Mrs. Pence left — and he bore a decorative well.

What d'you mean with the well there, Booper? I asked.

Lookit, he said. At some point the littlest one is goin' ta lose track of her baby doll. Me plan is to take the doll in question and — as a lesson, mind! — put her in your man the well and when the little one wants to know where her baby's gone to, I'll tell her that the liddle bairn's in the well, and that's what happens when you don't pay attention to a child of that age!

Booper, I said. That's horrible!

But that's just what he did, and it went just well as you would imagine.

Little Iphigenia invited myself, Tanit and the Pence family cat, Chief, to a tea party. Cucumber sandwiches and all the etiquette to beat the band, you understand. Right proper stuff. I even had me pocket watch set to the Greenwich Mean Time for the occasion.

But then where was Iphigenia's little baby; where could she be? She wanted to have tea like the rest, of course.

Why, Booper had thrown the babe in question down the well, just as he said he would. Well, there was a great hue and cry about the neighborhood with the end result being that I, Bryan O'Nolan — no solicitor, I — talked the neighbors out of arresting a man that both you know and that I know one Booper McCarthy for conspiracy to affray.

The end result was this: Booper and I had to find a way to take the Pence children out of town and entertain them until such time as their parents were to return. We were under too much suspicion and Booper was certain to bollox things up further. Luckily, I knew of a county fair some towns over where we could, I thought, keep the children fairly well entertained, fed and secure until Mr. and Mrs. Pence were ready to come home from Branson.

How wrong I was.

The five of us piled into Booper's out-of-service chicken truck and headed to the fair. I drove, of course, as the State of Indiana had long before asked Booper, in no uncertain terms, to never, ever, drive a vehicle.

When we arrived at the fair, we were waved around to the vendor entrance; presumably they thought the chicken truck was a going concern.

Bryan, Booper said. Don't you think they might feel we've gypped them out of our entrance fees?

Quiet, Booper! I tried to hush him. You can't go 'round usin' a word like that!

Which word?

G-Y-P-P-E-D, Booper, I spelled, keeping a close eye on the children in the back to see if they understood.

You know, I'm not much of a speller, Booper said.

Gah, man, the one about the gypsies.

Well, why not? Booper said. A noble race. Built the pyramids, they did. And that big sand dog that asks the riddles. Clever fellas, to be sure. Nothin' to be ashamed of, the Egypsies.

That's a myth, Booper, I said. They never did come from Egypt.

Is that why you can't talk about 'em, Bryan? The lyin' about be Egyptian?

No, Booper, you damn — the children gasped — dang fool! The term "gypped" is racially insensitive.

Booper screwed up his eyes.

I, I don't folla, he said.

Problematical?

What's that word? I don't know that one.

Why, I was sure you must, I said. It's quite current among the expensively under-educated, such as yourself. The word you used is bigoted,

Booper. It is a bigoted word.

Bigoted? he cried. Do you tell me so?

Indeed, I do, Booper, indeed, I do. It's based on a hurtful stereotype suggesting that these people you call gypsies regularly provide fraudulent services.

Like when me gran wanted her driveway paved, Booper said, and the pavers paved over her entire front garden and then charged her for the whole lot?

That's the sort of thing, yes, I said.

Why, those pavers were Italian! And Gran ended up thanking them for it, as now she has a better place to park her caravan!

Precisely what I'm tellin' ya about, Booper!

So what do we call 'em if we can't call 'em the other thing ya said, Bryan, the problematical thing?

"Roma people" is acceptable, I believe.

Roma? Like the tomatas? Do you tell me they're Italian, now, too?

Enough about the Italians, Booper, or I'll knock ya on the head!

I pulled us into a parking space.

Uncle Bryan, young Marmaduke said. Are those folks over there Roma people?

Ah, I'm glad you asked, lad, I said. I'm glad you asked. Those are carnival folk, sometimes called Carnies. They, too, have an uncouth reputation, but it's like I always say, judge the man on his character and not on the stereotypes of his people. Otherwise, you might think people like Booper and me were mere pugnacious idjits!

We brought the children into the fair. We had the fried dough; we saw your men the freaks in the freak show; we had our weights guessed — Booper had his six-foot frame correctly assessed at 13 stone; we watched as a man made an enormous quantity of the kettle corn, which we then ate; we saw all the chickens in the chicken barn, and we listened attentively to Booper's expostulations about the utility of each breed for eating.

He's always had strong opinions about such things.

It was when we got to the competition where the oxen try to pull ever-heavier objects that I realized that the girls, Tanit and Iphigenia, were missing.

Maimonides! I shouted.

Are you talking to me, Uncle Bryan? young Marmaduke said. My name is Marmaduke.

Of course it is! I said. Of course, Marmaduke, of course. Do you happen to know where your sisters are?

I haven't an idea, Uncle Bryan, said he. Uncle Booper gave me a couple of dead presidents to wager on that oxen team going next with that disheveled tramp in the corner who smells like Natural Lite and regret. My poor sisters! They've always been such obedient young ladies!

We need a plan! I said, ignoring for the time being that Booper had facilitated an introduction between Marmaduke and the wily gambler, Stanky the Tramp.

I have one! Marmaduke said. Uncle Booper, you search among the freaks; Uncle Bryan, you search the midway; I'll fellowship with the carnival folk!

An excellent plan, Marmaduke! I said. We meet back at the chicken truck!

He looked thrilled.

Which presidents, out of curiosity, Marmaduke?

Mostly Grant.

I see, I said. Let's be off!

We were off.

Was I alarmed by his adaptation of slang which would bring upon me the ire of Mr. and Mrs. Michael Pence? Yes. Was I concerned about his introduction to the cancerous world of gambling? Also, yes. Were either of these my priority in that moment? Not at all. Recovering Iphigenia and Tanit was the most important task I've been given since the time Michael asked me to arrange his socks alphabetically.

I headed to the midway. What sights and sounds would attract such young girls? My attempts at asking this directly of little girls and their parents was met with direct and specific obstruction such that I was warned by the site organizers never to return to the fair. I honestly thought that would have happened to Booper before it would happen to me.

I spotted a likely location immediately. The Cyclone ride was spinning madly. By the time I was able to get close I could see its riders were projectile vomiting as they rose and fell and spun. The nearby drink stand was covered in the stuff, dripping off like bile-colored rain.

Their cries were horrific.

Oh, the humanity!

I ran to the gate, only to have my deepest fears confirmed. There, at the controls, cackling madly was Tanit Pence. A man leapt over the fence and, with shocking placidity, asked her to stop the ride.

She did.

The riders, those capable of speech at any rate, were furious — the crowd that had gathered at the sight and smell beside themselves with anger and disgust — but the man calmed them all.

I am Dr. Betrand Quatermass, he said through a megaphone. This young lady is a hero! Were it not for her quick thinking you would all be in far worse shape, in the long run. Many of you might have been killed! You see, the ice cubes made at the soda shack which served you while you were in line for this ride contained dangerous levels of botulism! Lacking activated charcoal, the violent evacuation of your digestive systems was our only recourse.

Everyone within earshot — the exhausted riders, the shocked patrons, the carnival folk, the bearded lady on her 15 minute break, everyone

— cheered little Tanit as I lifted her onto my shoulders.

Doctor, I said, turning — but the doctor was gone.

Strange, that.

I met back up with Booper at the chicken truck as we'd planned.

I found he and little Iphigenia patiently explaining that — the truck being out of service — there were no wings to be had nor Scorchin' Skid Marks Sauce to dress them with to a line of disappointed carnival folk.

I say, Bryan, Booper said, you'd be proud of little Iffy, here. She and the Yak Lady are fast friends. That's where I found her, with the Yak Lady. Our friend here was described as a "kind, thoughtful and understanding companion."

Rather erudite, this Yak Lady, I said.

In my experience, they tend to be, Bryan, Booper said. Very wise, the Yak People. I imagine it's all that time they have for quiet contemplation, given that they are avoided by polite society.

I started up the truck.

That would explain your familiarity with them, Booper, not being a member of polite society yourself.

I suppose you're right, Bryan.

It wasn't until we were back at stately Pence Manor that we realized that Marmaduke wasn't with us.

Naturally, I panicked. The only thing I could

think to do was to call Dick Richards.

Dick, I said over the phone, can you come down to Mike's place? I've lost Melchizedek!

You mean Marmaduke? he said. I'll be right over.

It was an agonizing fifteen minutes waiting for him.

I got here as quickly as I could, Dick said. There was charcuterie everywhere.

Were you entertaining? Booper asked.

I'm always entertaining, Booper, he said with a wink. But I digress. The situation, briefly.

It is briefly thus, I said. We accidentally left Marmaduke at the fair.

Why haven't you returned to the fair? That's the first thing I'd do.

The fair is now closed and, to make matters worse, the carnival folk have packed up and moved off, destination unknown, presumably with Marmaduke in tow.

We need to search from the air, obviously.

Yes, but how, Dick? How?

Bryan, you may be the vastly more intelligent of the two adults left in charge here, but you can be incredibly dim sometimes.

And?

Our friend Michael is the owner of the 17th largest collection of classic autogyros in the world!

I did feel dim when Dick said that.

You're right, Dick. You're right. Let's get to the tarmac. Booper, you stay here and watch the girls.

Hey! Booper said as we left the house. That was offensive, Dick!

When we got to the tarmac, Dick told me that a travel agent friend of his had suggested that the carnival had most likely traveled west.

He jumped in an original Cierva C.6 while I took a Buhl A-1. We raced low towards the setting sun. Not half an hour later we saw the long, slow carnival snaking along the interstate. We flew ahead of the train and blocked all three lanes of the road with our autogyros.

While Dick went and negotiated Marmaduke's release, I stayed by our craft as a guard. Not only were the carnival folk angry, but there were enraged motorists to beat the band.

An irate policeman rode up on a motorcycle.

Now, Officer, I said. I can explain.

His face changed from anger to curiosity.

Hey, ain't you the guy who tracked down Dora the Explorer?

I am, I said, befuddled.

You know, that was some damn fine detective work. We use your report in trainings all the time. Textbook investigating.

Dick and Marmaduke ran up and jumped into the C.6.

We'll be going now, Dick shouted to the officer.

Well, he said to me. I'd ask for your

autograph, but I think a whole bunch of people would be mighty bent out of shape if I drew this out any longer.

I'll be sure to mention you in my book, Officer—?

Tingle's the name. Officer Brick Tingle.

Thank you, Officer Tingle. I must be off.

And off I was.

※ ※ ※

Michael and Mrs. Michael Pence were somewhat rather relieved when I'd finished the tale.

Marmaduke, why did you run off with the carnival folk? Mrs. Pence asked.

I was eager to learn their ancient ways, mother.

I hope you didn't learn too much about Stanky the Tramp and his ways, Michael said.

No, father.

Bryan, as to the autogiros —

Did you just say "autogiros," Michael? I asked. I've been saying "autogyros" this whole time.

They are, he said, homophones, in fact. They are spelled differently, but are pronounced the same. Cierva's original machines were called autogiros, but the general name for them now is autogyros. Like I said, different spelling, but the

same pronunciation.
I see.
Are the autogyros properly stowed?
Yes, of course. Dick took care of it.
Ah yes, Michael said. Good, old reliable Dick!

* * *

While you may think this story to be mere whimsy, the incident it describes has had a lasting effect on the Pence family, as Marmaduke Pence has grown up to become a lawyer and he founded the nation's premier Carny Anti-defamation organization.

7th March 2023

THE TIME MIKE TRIED TO MAKE SCOTTISHNESS GREAT AGAIN

Though we'd been long banned from volunteering from our good friend Mike Pence's political campaigns, when Booper and I heard that he was running for president and preparing for a first in the nation primary in New Hampshire we couldn't contain our excitement. We decided to help out in our own way and this story is, of course, a corker. Michael even changed his mind about our participation, though I'm not certain why. This story is even better than the one about the time Booper wrote a one act play about a student with a severe speech impediment attending Hogwarts. *Wingahblium Lebebosha*, he called it.

A disgrace and an insult to legitimate theater, I tell you.

Though we'd not kept up ourselves on the politics for quite a while, Booper and I put in what I'd say was yeoman's work "getting up to speed," as they say. We studied all the tricks, dirty and otherwise. The vote harvesting. The October surprises. PACs, of both the natural and Super varieties. Conjuring the dead for electoral success. We consulted an arcane magus on the subject of the campaign finance, from whose lectures we retired with only a dim understanding that if we were doing it and out of favor, we were probably doing it wrong. Then we heard about a magnificent way to bring people together: the identity politics, though I am certain that Booper's interest was driven entirely by his focus on the last two syllables of the politics in question.

At any rate, we went out to survey the good people of New Hampshire regarding our good friend Michael's name recognition using the identity politics in hopes that we might accidentally come up with that most insoluble of pancakes: an intersectional.

I am still ignorant as to what an intersectional is — some sort of grand divan or sofa I imagine — but that is the man that we were after.

Michael, I said, sat before a large easel in a conference room in his campaign headquarters in Manchester. Michael, we've found, understandably given that you are a recent vice president — no Schuyler Colfax or

Spiro Agnew, you! — that your name recognition is relatively consistent across the various demographical groups we surveyed.

Michael smiled and nodded.

The only group, I said, with any statistical ignorance of yourself, Michael, is that of the Scottish Americans.

Forsooth! Mike said, is it something — I daresay — Presbyterian?

His campaign manager, Charles McPherson, spoke up: It is not, Mr. Pence, if I may. I would go so far as to suggest that the Scottish American residents of New Hampshire might be quite keen to hear your forthright, plain speaking style. Your opposition to the Inclosure Acts will likely thrill the hearts of many.

But how might Michael reach so precise a demographic as this? I said.

There is a games — a Scottish games — he might visit, McPherson said. While it is in Vermont, it is put on by a New Hampshire concern and just over the border from the granite state. A tent could be acquired for such an event for a relatively modest investment. Besides, there are many points of interest: the highland athletics—

The you tell me what now? Highland athletics? said Booper.

Highland athletics, McPherson said. They are essentially understood as a series of athletic events based on an auld drunken wager. "I bet ye cannae throw this tree as far as I can, MacLeod." "I bet ye cannae carry or throw this rock as far as I can, Agnew." That sort of thing.

Hold up there, McPherson. Do you tell me that there is a clan Agnew? I said.

There is.

How serendipitous!

Mr. McPherson, Booper said, I would never call you any manner of dipitous, as my great friend Bryan just did, but tell me: Can a man as un-Scottish as myself compete in so erudite and effete events?

Booper, McPherson said, I've always considered you a great haggis of a man; you know the meaning of neither of those adjectives and besides, all are welcome at a highland games.

How interesting! Mike said. This might just be the sort of event that will get this campaign underw—

Here Michael paused in awkward trepidation.

Yes? said McPherson.

Oh, nothing! Mike said.

There obtained a pregnant silence.

So, McPherson, Michael said, you'll be spearheading this effort for us?

I will not, he said with decision. They insist on allowing, despite my repeated entreaties, Clan Campbell to attend.

But, Charles, Glen Coe was a long, long time ago!

I cleared me throat.

Not long enough for a Celt, I said.

※ ※ ※

Several weeks later, on the last Saturday of August, the campaign arrived at the grounds for the games. We had reserved a tent in the clan area after some negotiations with New Hampshire's founding Scottish-American arts organization.

Mike looked resplendent in his kilt.

Now, Michael, I asked. Can a man just wear any old tartan or is there some kind of system?

Hmm, he said. Yes and no. It is frowned upon to wear a tartan one does not have a family connection to, though anyone can wear the noble, famed and feared Black Watch.

And who are you wearing? asked Booper.

Ha! I've been asked that so many times! he said. Mother gave young Tanit a social studies assignment this last quarter to do some genealogical research on our family's history. It turns out that I am a direct descendant of Nial of the Nine Hostages, which endows me with the right to wear the tartan of Clan O'Niell. It is one of the half dozen or so Irish families to have a registered tartan, it turns out.

Michael, Booper said, it is lucky to have so noble an endowment.

Yes, friend Booper, I am lucky to be so well endowed and well do I know it.

We stood admiring Mike in his kilt, with his sporran fashioned out of a taxidermied badger and a tweed flat cap upon his head.

This would have come in handy when the family did our production of "The Scottish Play" last year, he said.

The what play? asked Booper.

We thespians don't say the name of the play as it is considered bad luck, Mike said.

But what's the play? Booper insisted.

The Scottish one; by Shakespeare.

Ah, Macbeth! Booper cried. Macbeth is one of me favorites. So Macbethy with all of your tomorrows and Macbeth and Lady Macbeth and the unsexing. Some men are Hamlet men, some cheer for Lear, but I'm a Macbeth man, through and through. I love Macbeth. It's even a fun word to say, Macbeth is. Macbeth!

Though not usually a superstitious man, a cloud of terror appeared to briefly darken Mike's countenance as Booper spoke.

We strode into the games. On one side of the track were displayed people dressed as ancient Picts, with wolfhounds, weapons, a peat fire and various implements of that long ago age.

Now I ask you, Michael, why would a person play dress up as a person with a thirty year life expectancy?

Oh, Bryan, it takes all kinds! They see their embrace of these folkways as educational. It's harmless!

I, for one, said Booper, would like to ride a wolfhound.

On the other side of the track there was a bound-off area for a sheepdog competition.

Do you tell me there is such a thing? Booper exclaimed. A sheepdog competition?

There is, and it is a delightful exhibition to observe, Booper, Mike said, I recommend it to you.

How fun! Booper replied, I may just take you up on the suggestion!

Which I knew he would, as I could see him counting off the difference between the current time and that of the competition on his fingers, a broad, if stupid, yet endearing smile occupying his face, his bitten tongue sticking out in mental exertion.

We came to the area where our paths would, for a time, fork.

Bryan, I must leave you, Mike said. I will join you anon at the clan tent. For now, I must go and give a workshop on tone when playing the *piobaireachd*.

The what?

The *ceòl mòr*; the great music of the highland pipes. As I now rank as an open professional I may no longer compete at this games, but I may judge and advise. And here I must leave you; I have a workshop to run! There will be massed bands at the end of the day, and I hope to march with them.

And off he went to tune his pipes.

Bryan, Booper said with concern in his voice, what sort of bands are these?

Why, the best kind: pipe and drum bands! I said.

Well, that's a relief! he said. My feelings on the brass bands are well known.

They are? I don't think even I have plumbed those depths with you, Booper.

My thoughts are these: The best thing that could happen to brass bands is that they all be melted down and made into bullet shells and church bells, bedam.

Booper went off to explore the food offerings while I — the very picture of confusion — wandered over to the Clan MacPence tent to encourage people to support Mike.

I donned a tee-shirt I'd had printed up for the occasion that said "Join Clan MacPence!" on the front. I had brochures, cards, pamphlets, stickers that said "Scots For Bonny Prince Mikey," commemorative plates, that sort of thing.

The response of the games's attendees was not what I'd expected, however.

It would appear that my exhortations to join Clan MacPence were interpreted as crass, inappropriate and, according to one elderly gentleman, "doon reet asinine."

He even called me a wanker!

I was thrice encouraged to perform an act of amorous congress upon myself. I was told

Michael couldn't hold a candle to the "laddie from Dunedin," whoever that is. A gentleman from Glasgow berated me for a quarter of an hour, though not a word did I understand.

I was all at sea. Things only got worse when an obviously thoroughly inebriated Booper McCarthy ran up. He looked terrible, despite the ludicrous grin his face wore.

Booper, man, what is wrong with you? I asked.

Nothing! I just ate an entire haggis, a half dozen of Scotch eggs, neeps and taddies by the pound and drank a baker's dozen of Tennent's! I won the caper toss! I've never been better!

Booper, I said, come here and let me get you back on the primrose path to sobriety.

Can't, he shouted, running off. I've entered meself in the sheepdog competition! Remember the porter!

I'd no idea what he meant, but I was too busy fighting off a woman arguing against the premise of my "Make Scottishness Great Again!" bumper stickers to dedicate any attention to the matter.

Mike rescued me moments later.

My fellow Celts! he intoned and the crowd quieted to listen. I apologize if my campaign has offended your sensibilities. This was not my intention or the intention of my campaign. It was simply out of love — of fellowfeeling, you see! — that I asked my staff to reach out to the organizers of this games in order to put up a Clan MacPence tent. I thought the name scanned lithely and functioned neatly as a pun on my own name. Clan Mike Pence, do you see? Whether you see or not is unimportant. What is important is my contrition, my genuine supplication for your forgiveness. Can you, the people of this games, forgive me?

Michael had won the crowd over to his side. If they did not support him, they at least understood him.

Then Booper arrived.

Up the hill he came running, pursued by a slobbering wolfhound, an angry mob of Picts and a flock of sheep driven by all of the dogs of the sheepdog competition operating like the individual instruments in an orchestra. Arvo Pärt himself could not orchestrate so full a pursuit.

Booper tumbled into our tent and the angry mob was calling for blood.

It was then that a lady — white haired, she was, a lady of experience and age and driving a golf cart — parted the crowd like Moses himself and pulled up to our tent, the table which had stood before it certain not to return its deposit to Michael's campaign.

She narrowed her eyes.

I think you need to leave, she said in even and uncompromising tones.

Ma'am, Mike said, I think you're right.

However, she said, before you go, Mr. McCarthy has earned this for his performance in the caber toss.

She handed over a medal emblazoned with the word "participant."

Booper paraded about in it, all aglow, for the following fortnight.

20th May 2023

A VICTORY OF ILLOGIC, A COMEDY OF ERRORS

It doesn't take a Nostradamnus to foretell that a story about a then-future vice president — particularly such a one as Mr. Michael Pence — being chased by armed security guards is going to be a good one. Now, I don't recall any of your men the armed security guards being harmed in the incident and I've no doubt they never have put the two and two together and realized that the target of their chase was none other than Michael and his two stalwart companions, the tragically late Booper McCarthy and myself.

It all began at Señor Bubbles, the local soda fountain, where we met on a Sunday. I remember that it was a Sunday because Michael showed up with a copy of Pastor Dennis's 500,000 word sermon on the allegedly ungodly trend of keeping capybaras as pets. I do not recall this fad but my copy of the sermon kept my house warm for over a fortnight. Needless to say, the Pences never owned any of your men the capybaras.

Anyhow, Michael was in a mood: He and Mrs. Pence had just purchased their first home. He tried his best to appear enthusiastic at the prospect.

Nothing grand, he said, but it has one and a half baths and—

These half baths, Booper interrupted, are they so oriented that you can only wash your top half or bottom, or your starboard half or port, if you get my meaning?

Booper— Mike began.

Is an idjit, I said. The half baths have a sink and no more than that and a toilet.

Toilet? I thought they'd painted it! Booper exclaimed.

Actually, Friend Bryan, one of them has — and here he whispered, lest he be overheard — a b-i-d-e-t.

They eat the what, now? Booper said incredulously.

Would you shut it, man, or we'll never get this tour out of the latrines! I said in exasperation.

I'm just happy to have a place with a landing pad for storks, Mike said. A happy domicile.

A domicile? Booper said, scratching his head and squinting his eyes in the deepest depths of befuddlement. Does that mean you've been domesticated, Michael?

Mike looked crestfallen.

It does feel that way, at times. I worry, friends, he admitted, that this may be a symbolic end to our days of high adventure.

Well, Michael, when do you close on the digs? I said.

In a month or so, Bryan, why do you ask?

I think there's at least one last adventure left on the horizon. What have you always wanted to see?

Well, I don't know, Bryan. Has the State Department seen fit to reinstate Booper's passport?

Sadly, they have not, I said.

It's understandable, considering the trauma suffered by the animals of *Zoologico Guadalajara*. I think, friends, that what I'd like to see is the site of an epoch-defining disaster. While I'll — God willing! — never witness such a thing in person, I would like to observe its effects first hand. I think our destination shall be the Barringer Crater in Arizona.

No sooner had he spoken it into being then were we loading the last of our luggage into what was once Booper's chicken wing food truck.

Thank you for accommodating us, Friend Booper, Michael said. Mother is having my woodie detailed as a birthday present.

No worries! Booper said. We'll just have to

fight off demands for wings with my signature Regretful Colon sauce. No small task, that!

We're all familiar with the mercurial nature of your colon, Booper, Mike said.

And with that we were off on our grand adventure. In no time, it seemed, we were on the I-40 outside of Joseph City, Arizona, pulling over for gas and directions.

Booper and I were in charge of snacks.

What I find ironical is that our friends the Slim Jims, Booper said, holding two fistfuls of the meat sticks in question, are named after an implement for the opening o fa locked car door and yet they themselves have packaging that could foil the most professional of automobile thieves.

An uncharacteristically astute observation, I said, embracing the convenience store's entire stock of Andy Capp's Cheddar Fries.

It was then that we saw Mike approaching us with a frown and several bottles of mineral water.

What is it, Michael? I said.

The attendant, Bryan, tells me that the crater is closed and, as such, he will not tell me the way there. I'd like to find it anyway — perhaps we can see it from a distance — yet I've no idea how to proceed.

Did you remonstrate with him, Michael?

Of course, Bryan.

But did you remonstrate with him vigorously, Michael?

As vigorously as decorum would allow. In fact, I promised him a sternly worded letter on the subject to follow.

We paid for our snacks and drinks, treating the attendant as gruffly as we could without crossing the social Rubicon into open disdain, and outside of the truck I confronted Michael.

Now, Michael, I said, I'm not being in any manner critical of yourself or your ways; you are the very picture of a modern man, if not a major general. Your problem, in this discrete instance, is that you've approached our dilemma *logically*. I would suggest that in this, as in most other situations, you'd be well advised to think and do as I do, for I am not a student of logic, but rather am I a great student of the *illogic*.

Bryan, Booper said, I don't folla.

I imagine not, my great friend. Your men the logicians, your students of the logic, have very strange ways. An example for your edification: the Barber's Paradox: You see, there's a remote village beyant with only a solitary barber for the whole congregation. This fella the barber has a peculiar rule, so say the logicians, in that he will only shave the faces of men who will not shave the faces of others. Who, then — so ask your men the logicians — shaves the barber? They think they have you there, but the solution is obvious: Either the barber's mother does it for him or, more likely, I think you'll agree, the barber — the very author of this absurd and unnecessary rule — wears himself a beard!

Michael and Booper looked upon me with suspicious curiosity.

Another example, my dear friends, I said. There's a barbershop wherein three barbers live and work. They are yclept Archer, Bowyer and Carver; the last is the preferred of the three. The shop is always open — why, in God's name, would they be shaving their fellow man at three o'clock in the morning, we'll never know — but such, we are told by the logicians, is the case. Also, your man Archer is a paranoid and will not go out unless he's accompanied by Bowyer. At this one of your men who wants to be shaved by Carver exclaims that he can logically prove that your man Carver must be in! This paradox was proposed by the brilliant mathematician who wrote the book about the girl and the rabbit in the waistcoat with the pocket watch.

Ah, Michael said, Lewis—

Jabberwocky! Booper shouted.

That's the fella! I exclaimed. At any rate, the clear solution is that either Carver can be in, or Archer and Bowyer can be in, or just Archer can man the shop by himself! I fail to understand why supposedly brilliant people — who were clearly much smarter than the man that you know and that I know, one Bryan O'Nolan — could fail to see such an obvious solution.

Was it all about your men the barbers with these logical fellas, then, Bryan? Booper said.

Yes, the barbers and sentient turtles chatting up Achilles.

What did the turtle say to Achilles? Booper said.

Lookit, I said, we could be at this until kingdom come. Let me give you a further example. Your smart men the logicians will suggest that the temperature is both ninety degrees on the Fahrenheit scale—

Ah, the Fahrenheit. As God intended, Booper said, elbowing Michael and giving a knowing nod.

And, I continued, rising.

Did you learn all this at Le Cordon Bleu, Bryan?

I did indeed, I said. These logicians will hold that the temperature is ninety degrees. They will then hold that the temperature is rising. They will tertiarily hold that the temperature must be then both rising and ninety.

Hm, Michael said.

The premise is this, Michael, I said. The temperature is ninety degrees Fahrenheit — if it were not the Fahrenheit everyone would be dead — second, the temperature is rising. Thus, so say the logicians, that the temperature is simultaneously ninety degrees and rising. Bollocks, all bollocks! The temperature can only be ninety degrees and rising from that temperature!

In point of fact, I continued, the propositions themselves are not remotely compatible. The first, "The temperature is ninety degrees Fahrenheit," I'll take for granted. That we are not conceiving a world in which humans are either flash-frozen or sublimating like the Wicked Witch of the West, the system in question is thus warm, bordering on hot, given individual taste. The second proposition is "The temperature is rising." Thus the syllogism, Michael and Booper, "The temperature is ninety degrees and also rising," is false.

How could your conclusion be demonstrated, Michael said, as you say illogically?

It's all the "the temperature is this" and "the temperature is also that" nonsense. What they don't understand is this: In the first proposition, "The temperature is 90 degrees," your man 90 is a workaday noun. He comes into the sentence, does his job like he's supposed to and off to the missus for a simple but satisfying supper. Does he expect a parade in his honor, our friend 90? He does not, begob! Then comes this flash fella called Rising. He'll be the first to tell ya he's no mere noun but a gerund, do you understand, a verb condescending from the high state of action to take the part of Noun in our play. Now, the logicians, mere groundlings in the theater of thought, cannot tell the difference! They think them both nouns! I will say this for your man the gerund: He always retains a whiff of action about him and he is right to say that he and a noun like 90 are not the same. If not apples and oranges, your men the logicians are comparing apples and, well, crabapples!

You astound me, Bryan, Michael said.

Another! The Liar's Paradox: "This sentence is false." No better proof of the existence of God and the folly of Man can you find in the land of the living. The logician cannot make sense of his proposition. He fails to understand all which exists outside of his so-called logic. Better yet, he fails to understand that logic is, in itself, fallacious: It presupposes its own existence!

I proffered a shoe box.

One more for you, Michael, Schrödinger's Cat: The cat in this box is both living and dead, until one opens the box and confirms the case one way or the other, so says the logician.

I handed the box in question to Michael.

This box has a distinct purring sound coming from within, he said. And the contents appear to be moving of their own accord.

Precisely! Your men the logicians would have told you that opening the box determined whether or not your fella the cat was living or dead!

Bryan, do you just carry around a kitten in a box all the time?

I'll not address such calumny, Michael, I said. It is neither here nor there. I merely propose that we should approach our dilemma in the most illogical way possible.

What do you propose?

Here's what I suggest we do, I said. We drive

off in any direction other than the one from which we came and we see what we can see.

And so we did: We drove off across the desert, sand and dust tossed up by our tires like a series of slow, unending waves thrown in parallel paths behind us. The desert sun shone on our chicken truck speeding across the wastes of Arizona as if we were three fugitives from justice blessed with the chicken truck aforesaid and an abiding yearning for freedom.

Soon we saw an apparent rise in the land before us with a chain link fence separating ourselves from it.

We came to realize, as the fence and rise grew before us, that what we were seeing was the great wall of the Barringer Crater himself.

We brought the truck to a stop and approached the paling separating us from the majesty of the site of the age-altering conflagration — the meteorite — which struck our toddling Earth some 50 millennia ago.

We approached the fence, its barbed spikes reaching out above our heads, gravid with awe.

Behold, said Michael, behold, my friends Bryan and Bernard, the power of God.

We were silent for time out of time as we stared into the crater, a vast bowl of infinite browns, golds and weathered tans.

Michael? Booper said.

Yes, Booper?

D'you think that's some sort of village

or settlement down there on the crater floor, Michael? Just there in the shadows?

Heck-o, Molly! Michael said with great enthusiasm, I believe it just might be!

Think we could go down there, Michael? Booper said. I have to use the jakes.

Now, Michael, I said, I know you'll find this shocking, but I agree with Booper, despite the clear violation of laws Federal, State and Local it would be to do it.

And it was then that Michael uttered, under that clear, cerulean Arizona sky, what might be the nine strangest words I have ever known him to utter: Yes, let's; I, too, need to use the jakes.

The problem, Michael, as I see it, is how to surmount your man the fence.

If only we had some bolt cutters! Mike exclaimed, striking his palm with his fist.

We three thought hard, each to his own ability.

Michael, Booper began, would bolt cutters be the class of character you might use to separate the three parts of the chicken wing into sections?

What do you mean?

Well, there's your man the flat, his friend the drumette and the leftover bit that hangs around at the end but doesn't really contribute much.

A finer— I began.

Quiet, Bryan, Michael said. Friend Booper might be onto something. Booper, do you have one of these wing separators in your truck?

I should have, yes, he said.

The sun drooped westward.

Might you be willing to go and get them?

Of course, Booper cried. Why didn't you say so?

He ran off to the truck, from which then came a great series of bangs and clangs and ringings interspersed with exclamations of pain from the searching Booper within. He emerged, eventually, with a pair of bolt cutters, the handles of which seemed to be covered in dried-on hot sauce.

Booper, Mike said, eyeing the handles, I think you should have the honor of cutting the fence, as the author of our breakthrough.

A few skillful snips later and we found ourselves sneaking down the face of the crater serpentine-style to the floor some 600 feet below.

You fellas amaze me, I said as we set foot on the crater's bottom. For two gents who needed to use the gents at the top, I find myself the only one in apparent urinal distress!

Mike looked sheepish.

I may have wetted some of the stony loam of the Winona series shortly after we began ascending the outer rim of the crater.

I signed me name on that boulder beyant, Booper said with a broad smile. The one that says "Bernard" on it, that's mine.

Well, Bryan, Michael began, why don't

Booper and I face away from you and gaze at this settlement not a third of a mile from us in the shadow of the crater's rim while you relieve yourself.

So I turned around, undid me trousers and beheld such a fright as I've seldom had before.

Oh, no, Michael— I stammered.

Do you need Booper and me to make susurrous murmurings like the tinkles of a running faucet draining gently into a sink to assist you?

No, Michael, I said. We're not alone!

We'd been spotted by security at the crater's rim! We could hear their wordless shouts.

Gentlemen, Michael said with icy calm, there's no time to lose.

And off we ran to the settlement, the shouts fading — but never quite into silence as we ran — behind us.

When we breathless reached it, the settlement was a stark little community, all green and full of live in contrast to the crater's earthy age. It had quiet bungalows with small squares of artificial turf before them, walkable neighborhoods, restaurants and services all conveniently located and plentiful bike paths. And all abustle into the bargain. A planner's paradise!

What's more, it was filled with familiar faces. We even saw Jimmy Hoffa!

Michael, I said, what is this place, some sort of celebrity retreat?

His face was shrouded with suspicion and did not answer.

We walked down a sidewalk — always keeping to the shady side, if possible — which appeared to take us to the town center.

A man approached us with a great smile and the face of a long-sitting senator I shall not name. He walked directly up to Michael with his hand outstretched.

Ezra! I haven't seen you in a month of Sundays, he said. I've been terribly busy with — here he gave a deep wink — you-know-what lately and I just haven't had a chance to swing by! Perhaps Phyllis and I will on Friday. I hope that tuna is still on the menu — here another wink — well, I must be off.

And, indeed, off he was.

Between Michael, Booper and I, a more confounded trio you could not find in all of Barringer Crater, I'd wager.

Michael, what was all that about?

Why, I've no idea, he said.

It was not a quarter of an hour later that we had another, similarly strange, encounter, this time with a star of screen and television that I've no doubt you would recognize.

Well, hello, Ezra, she said. Never thought I'd see you more than two blocks from the joint.

Michael was flustered, so I jumped into the conversation.

That is exactly our problem, Madam, if you

understand. We've wandered off and now can't find our way back to this joint you speak of.

Oh, no worries! Just take a left at the next intersection and then three streets down, at the intersection of Bilderberg Way and Trilateral Course.

And thus it was, at the intersection of those very streets, that we saw it in brightest neon: Pence-&-a-Cola Pizza.

All eyes were upon us as we entered. We strode to the bar, where a man who looked like an aged sketch of D.B. Cooper was wiping down tumblers.

His eyes widened when he saw Michael.

Boss, you got that important phone call that's gonna start any minute now, git back in yer office!

And so he pushed and shuffled and shoved the three of us through the kitchen and into a small, dark back office, the door shut firmly behind us.

There was a man at a desk in the office. He wore the coat of a chef and was the spit of Mike Pence himself. He rose to attention.

Mr. Pence, he said, this is unexpected.

To me as well, Michael said, who are you, and what is going on here?

My name is Ezra Yirmeya, the pseudo-Pence said. This is Their secret facility for storing body doubles. Any time They need a body double for some conspiracy or another, they come here. This is only the surface level, of course. There are many more below ground.

Are you telling me, sir, I said, that there's a body double for anyone they think they might need?

Oh course, he said with a laugh, you can't just go putting an ad for a body double in the newspaper when you need one, can you? No, we're held here until we are needed.

It seems like a pleasant enough place, Michael ventured.

It's a prison, it doesn't matter how good the food is.

Mike recounted how we had to break in and were pursued.

Inmates still tried to escape Alcatraz, despite its high culinary reputation, I said.

I feel a moral obligation, then, to give my body double his freedom, if he wants it.

He does, Mr. Yirmeya said, pounding the table.

The phone rang.

I think I can get us out, if you can get me somewhere to hide, he said.

Mike nodded; the would-be Mike picked up the phone.

Yeah, he said into the receiver. Sounds like a neat little job. I'll need three normies to help me out, but I think I can arrange that. Drop me at the Crater Welcome Center.

He hung up the phone.

So while I get you a disguise, Mr. Pence, you

get me a hiding spot.

Soon Mike was wearing a very lifelike, and may I say very fetching, handlebar mustachio and a ten gallon hat.

Are you really a chef? Michael asked.

Classically trained. I leave behind two Michelin stars with this escape.

Then why don't you move in with Mother and me and be my personal chef? It'll be the perfect hiding spot, so long as there's no confusion on Mother's part! Wouldn't want to cause a scandal!

I don't think you have to worry about me corrupting Mrs. Pence, Ezra said.

No, Mike said, I'm worrying she'll mistake you for me, you handsome devil!

That's not really my, shall we say, area of interest.

Mike was very confused.

Think he's telling you that he's a homosexual, Michael, I said.

Oh! Mike exclaimed. A homosexual in the culinary world? The Food Network led me to believe that American restaurants were positively bristling with near-toxic masculinity! Well, that is no matter then. Let us get you to your freedom, Mr. Yirmeya. What is your plan?

It is this: You and your friends came to this crater even though it is closed. You therefore have some mode of transportation we could use once we get to the top. As long as they don't recognize you are the interlopers — after all, they only saw you at a distance — we can make good our escape. Foolproof, right?

Michael and I let our gaze fall on one Booper McCarthy.

Everything was going fine until two security guards approached us as we climbed into the food truck. One of them was carrying Booper's discarded bolt cutters.

Why, one of them said, I've been havin' a hankerin' for hot wings all afternoon.

Well, Booper said through the window, I don't—

Can I at least have a sample of that Sri Lankan Hornet Pepper Sauce?

Oh, Booper recovered, of course!

He poured a sample into a little cup and handed it over to the guard.

The guard dipped his finger in the sauce and touched it to his tongue. His eyes went from the sauce to the handles of the bolt cutters to the truck.

Hey, ain't you fellas the ones who broke into the crater earlier?

Look my friend, I said, you can say what you want about the internal combustion engine and its connection to climate change, but it has given us one of nature's truly beautiful, if ephemeral, phenomena: the sight of a thin sheet of ice atop a box truck catching the wind on the highway and peeling up and then splintering and crashing to the Earth and shattering as if it had never been.

What are you talking about?

We'll need a higher class of illogic, if we're to escape this one, Bryan, Michael said. Oh no, he shouted, pointing behind the guards and into the crater as Ezra started the engine. Vazooleyhorns! he cried.

The moment they'd turned their backs was just enough for Ezra to get the truck moving and ourselves on our way back to Indiana.

It was somewhere in Oklahoma that Mike turned to Booper and me from the driver's seat — Ezra was asleep in the back, using a sack of Booper's Chicken Truck promotional t-shirts as a pillow — and said, Fellows, it's escapades like these that make me hope that there will always be another adventure sat just over the horizon.

❄ ❄ ❄

Some time I should tell you about why Booper and I are no longer welcome in the White House Rose Garden.

30th June 2023

About the Author

Bryan O'Nolan is a white-bearded writer living in New Hampshire. He resembles the narrator of this work as much as its subject resembles its real-world counterpart. When not writing or editing, he wishes he were. He is a dedicated believer in the difference between countable and non-countable nouns and staunch opponent of Oxford comma absolutism. He is an editor for Ordinary Times.

Made in United States
North Haven, CT
06 July 2023